The Plough and the Stars

with notes for students by Christopher Murray

Sean O'Casey was born in Dublin in 1880. He was the youngest of seven surviving children and, because of malnutrition, ill health and poverty, he had little formal education. Although the first half of his life was spent as a labourer, he involved himself with the Irish political struggle for both independence and the betterment of conditions for the poor. He was secretary of the Irish Citizen Army, and wrote for the *Irish Worker*. The production at the Abbey Theatre of his early plays, including *The Plough and the Stars*, translated his experiences into art and brought him international acclaim. Like many another great Irish writer, he paid his country the compliment of leaving it as soon as he conveniently could. Having lived in London and Chalfont St Giles, in 1938 he moved with his young family to Devon, where he died in 1964.

Christopher Murray is Associate Professor of Drama and Theatre History at University College, Dublin. His publications include *Twentieth-Century Irish Drama: Mirror Up to a Nation* (Manchester, 1997), *Brian Friel: Essays, Diaries, Interviews 1964–1999* (Faber, 1999) and *A Faber Critical Guide to Sean O'Casey: The Shadow of a Gunman, Juno and the Paycock, The Plough and the Stars* (Faber, 2000).

SEAN O'CASEY

The Plough and the Stars

with notes for students by
CHRISTOPHER MURRAY

faber and faber

This edition first published in 2001
by Faber and Faber Limited
74–77 Great Russell Street
London WC1B 3DA

Reprinted 2016

First published by Macmillan London Ltd in 1926
Reprinted in *Sean O'Casey: Plays Two*
by Faber and Faber Limited, 1998

Typeset by Country Setting, Kingsdown, Kent CT14 8ES
Printed in the UK by CPI Group (UK) Ltd, Croydon CR0 4YY

A CIP record for this book
is available from the British Library

ISBN 978-0-571-21232-3

4 6 8 10 9 7 5

Contents

Introduction to Sean O'Casey

There are some writers whose personalities and life-histories are so attractive that we find ourselves drawn to them and captivated even before taking their work into account. Sean O'Casey was one of those writers. An underdog all his life and without benefit of more than the most basic education, O'Casey spoke out loudly and often on all matters to do with human rights. Born into poverty, he always sympathised with the poor and the underprivileged. He became not only a playwright of the people but a constant commentator, in letters to the newspapers and in articles for magazines, on injustices of every kind. Indeed, it would hardly be too much to say that O'Casey's whole life and career were dedicated to opposing injustice wherever and whenever he saw it.

But every writer is governed and moulded by the time and place in which he or she is born and brought up. When O'Casey was born in Dublin on 30 March 1880, that city was still a British colony ruled from Westminster. As a Protestant, O'Casey (or, as his name was before he gave it a Gaelic spelling, 'John Casey') was automatically unionist in politics. Even though working class (Michael Casey was a clerk), the Casey family saw themselves as apart from the Roman Catholic majority, who were for the most part nationalists in favour of Home Rule for Ireland. O'Casey might have settled himself comfortably into lower-middle-class Dublin life by using the advantages of his Protestant connections, even though, being poor, he lacked the privileges which allowed fellow-Dubliners Synge and Wilde to attend Dublin University (Trinity College); to be Protestant in Dublin one hundred years ago was at least to be on the winning side. But poverty, especially after his father's death when the boy was only six years old, and the eye disease trachoma seriously stunted O'Casey's development. He had only three years' education up to the age of fourteen, but benefited from his older sister Bella's qualifications as a teacher. After that, while working on and off in lowly jobs in Dublin businesses in his teenage years, O'Casey educated himself by reading all the books that he could lay his hands on and his painful eyesight would allow him to study. In particular, he steeped himself in the Bible – a requirement of his Sunday-school class – and Shakespeare (O'Casey's brother was a part-time actor). Finding that Dublin libraries were ill-stocked in the materials which interested him most, O'Casey formed the habit of buying cheap editions of the great authors in the second-hand bookstores. A love of learning, often the most powerful fuel of the would-be writer, was thus early fostered. Ever afterwards O'Casey was a voracious reader, not just in dramatic literature (where Shaw became a favourite alongside Shakespeare) but also in poetry, religious studies, art and music. It is no surprise that the characters in his plays to whom O'Casey is most sympathetic are usually those who strive to lift themselves out of a restrictive environment through reading. Later in life, O'Casey wrote essays on the writers he most admired: Shakespeare, Ibsen, Gorki, Shaw, Synge, Yeats, and many more. The view he adhered to all his life was that books were for all, not just for the educated, and that they were as important to the working person as bread on the table.

When regular office employment of any kind proved impossible for O'Casey (mainly because he could not put up with the grovelling to authority it seemed to require), he took up hard manual labour with the Dublin railways. He enjoyed the outdoor work with pick and shovel but when he insisted on his right to join a trade union in 1911 he was dismissed. From that time on, until his plays began to make money, O'Casey could get work only occasionally, and he lived a simple hard life with his mother Susan on little more than her old-age pension until she died in November 1918. He then set about making his living as a writer, first of popular verse, then as historian of the Irish Citizen Army (which had fought without his help in the 1916 Easter Rising) and eventually, from 1923, as a playwright for the Abbey Theatre in Dublin. Once his plays proved successful enough to be accepted in London he went to live there and never again worked at anything else but full-time writing.

The rejection by the Abbey Theatre of his anti-war play *The Silver Tassie* in 1928 led O'Casey into more experimental work. It is often said that the break with the Abbey, where he had learned his trade, was tragic for O'Casey; in any event, although *Within the Gates* (1934) and *The Star Turns Red* (1940) were brave experiments, these and other later plays were not successful on the London stage. By this time O'Casey was fully committed to Communism, although never a member of the party, and this commitment increasingly told against him. His first biographer, David Krause, has described O'Casey as 'a moral pacifist as well as a militant socialist', and this accurately sums up O'Casey's political position. It is little wonder that when the English theatre underwent a revolution in 1956 and angry new writers emerged, they showed their admiration for O'Casey by writing in a somewhat similar, realistic but anti-establishment mode. There was thus a renewal of interest in O'Casey's plays around 1960, by which time he was eighty years old and close to death. So far as most critics of modern drama are concerned, O'Casey's best work was complete with *The Plough and the Stars*, written almost forty years before his death in Torquay, Devon, in September 1964. But he himself always insisted that his later, experimental, plays were better.

The material of the three Dublin plays – *The Shadow of a Gunman, Juno and the Paycock* and *The Plough and the Stars* – owes a lot to O'Casey's experience as a young man involved in Irish political and cultural life. From about 1906 he was a member of the Gaelic League where he learned the Irish language, first changed his name, and became fiercely nationalistic. He joined the Irish Republican Brotherhood not long afterwards and rejoiced in writing anti-British propaganda. But when Jim Larkin (1882–1947) arrived in Dublin from Liverpool and set about creating an active trade-union movement, O'Casey began to abandon all religious, cultural and republican organisations in favour of socialism. The great lock-out of 1913, which saw thousands of Dublin manual workers in opposition to the bosses controlling the transport and distribution industries and services, showed O'Casey that the cause of labour took precedence over the cause of Irish freedom. He was appointed secretary of the Irish Citizen Army which Larkin formed in 1914 for the defence of the workers and for a while he was active in administration. But, characteristically, he was unable to reconcile his own views with those of the majority and resigned in 1914 on a policy matter. O'Casey was thus isolated by the time of the 1916 Rising. He became a spectator of Irish political life when he might have been a major participant.

The 1916 Rising, led by Pádraic Pearse (Commandant, Irish Volunteers) and James Connolly (Commandant, Irish Citizen Army), was an abortive one. It took place in some confusion on Easter Monday 1916 following an attempt by the chief of staff of the Irish Volunteers (Eoin MacNeill) to cancel the proceedings. Pearse and Connolly, in defiance of MacNeill, led a revolt which failed to spread outside the city of Dublin. No more than 2,000 men in all participated, taking over the General Post Office and other strategic sites in Dublin. This heroic but foolhardy undertaking, marred by indecision, poor communications, lack of firepower, and lack of general support, was easily crushed by British forces within a week. Pearse, Connolly and thirteen other leaders were summarily executed. It was these executions that changed the political climate in Ireland and precipitated the guerilla war of independence which led to the signing of the Treaty between Britain and Ireland in 1921, and the establishment of a twenty-six-county Free State in the South.

O'Casey, while admiring the courage of those who fought in 1916, saw the enterprise as a waste of life and effort. In particular, he faulted Connolly for deflecting the cause of labour into a nationalist struggle. By making an alliance between the Irish Citizen Army and the Irish Volunteers under Pearse, Connolly had, in O'Casey's analysis, betrayed the true purpose of the Irish Citizen Army and taken part in a charade. He makes this point in his *Story of the Irish Citizen Army* (1919). O'Casey's attitude towards the Rising, then, tended to be critical and condemnatory. By this time, and especially after the 1917 Russian Revolution (which he applauded), nationalism was for him a delusion.

This was not always the case. His early writings, journalistic pieces and poems, were unashamedly republican in theme and language. After 1913 his writings became more socialist than nationalist but were still propagandist in style. It is indeed remarkable that such a fanatic as O'Casey's early writings show him to have been (as evidenced in the collection of his early work entitled *Feathers from the Green Crow*) should ever have grown into a major dramatic artist. There is something miraculous about this shift in direction, though 'fate' and O'Casey's character no doubt were other factors. But the three Dublin plays are like the great war poems written by Owen, Sassoon and others: they would not have anything like their impact and intensity were it not for the author's personal and complex experience, which rendered them pacifist in outlook.

O'Casey's plays are distinctively modern and, as an Abbey playwright, he more or less adopted realism as a matter of course. But his plays are much freer in structure than the three-act realistic play usually demands: O'Casey prefers to work from life, combining a scanty plot with character sketches with 'turns' reminiscent of the music hall. At times O'Casey's use of the group, the ensemble, in preference to the individual hero, is reminiscent of Chekhov's style, for example in *Three Sisters* (1901). But O'Casey's world, the world he creates on stage, is vastly different from Chekhov's, which is invariably sophisticated, intellectually advanced, and poised ready to fall apart. O'Casey's is a more robust, devil-may-care, down-to-earth world, where the working-class characters struggle to survive. O'Casey abolishes the hero in favour of the anti-hero. In doing so, he introduces a good deal of irony and even satire into the dramatic action.

O'Casey extended the Irish tradition in ways which were to affect how the modern theatre developed. The Abbey players who brought his plays on to the London and New York stages in the late 1920s and early 1930s were among the best of their generation and included Barry Fitzgerald, Sara Allgood and F. J. McCormick. Their ensemble-playing held lessons for repertories all over the world. Also, the plays themselves, in their combination of tragedy and comedy to form a new and modern tragi-comedy, pointed the way for many twentieth-century writers from John Osborne to Edward Bond. These later writers looked back with great respect to O'Casey's pioneering work, for they too were trying to find ways of using the stage to combine entertainment and criticism of social and political values. Samuel Beckett, whose political outlook was as different from O'Casey's as his Dublin origins, nevertheless admired and may even have imitated O'Casey's use of knockabout farce within the tragic situation.

As time passed, O'Casey's three Dublin plays became part of the world repertoire of twentieth-century drama. Indeed, opinion elevated Sir Laurence Olivier's 1966 production of *Juno* at the National Theatre in London into one of the best ever seen. Further, the representation of the long-suffering mother, Juno, was to be imitated by many playwrights, including the American Clifford Odets and the British Arnold Wesker. O'Casey's depiction of warfare, particularly in its urban, guerilla aspects, showed many other writers how best to dramatise politics: by uniting simple home or domestic life with the world of political violence. This link between private and public was the means of showing cause and effect and how people's lives can be torn apart by the forces which invade and conflict with their happy, careless routines.

Finally, it needs to be emphasised that O'Casey, far from being a narrow, politically biased playwright, always shows the deepest compassion for the sufferings of his characters. Indeed, it would not be too much to say that O'Casey's plays, while dealing with issues of life and death, are invariably and enthusiastically on the side of life.

REFERENCES

Krause, David, 'The Maiming of Sean O'Casey', *Sean O'Casey Review*, ed. Robert Lowery, 3.2 (Spring 1977), p. 137.

O'Casey, Sean, *The Autobiographies*, 6 books, published in 2 vols., London: Macmillan, 1963.

—— *Red Roses for Me*, in *Sean O'Casey: Plays One*, London: Faber and Faber, 1998.

The Abbey Theatre

The theatre for which O'Casey first wrote was the Abbey in Dublin. Founded in 1904 by the poet W. B. Yeats (1865–1939), the playwright and administrator Lady Gregory (1852–1932) and the poet and playwright John Millington Synge (1871–1909), the Abbey from the outset was a brave and combative little theatre. Its origins lay in two impulses which were not always in harmony and when in opposition created explosive audience reaction.

One impulse was to create a theatre of art along the lines of the new 'free' or 'independent' theatres in London, Paris, Berlin and, perhaps most famously, Moscow. There was a common idea stretching right across Europe from the late 1880s, namely to oppose the commercial, conventional theatre of the nineteenth century, with its star system, its reliance on spectacular scenery and sensational effects to create the maximum illusion, and its cultivation of worn-out dramatic styles (as seen in the 'well-made play' in particular). The Independent Theatre established in London in 1891 probably first gave Yeats the idea of providing an alternative theatre for Dublin, where similar conditions were in place. Indeed, Yeats himself contributed an early play to the Independent Theatre in 1894, sharing the double bill with Shaw's *Arms and the Man*. Shaw, however, was a lot more interested in using the Independent Theatre to create a new drama similar to the realistic plays of Ibsen (1828–1906), such as *A Doll's House* (1879) and *Ghosts* (1881). Yeats was rather more interested in Symbolism, and in the new poetic plays he had seen or read in Paris. He had serious doubts about the value of realism, and hoped to control its development in favour of a restoration of poetic drama to the stage. However, the spread of naturalism – an extreme form of realism – across Europe culminated in the establishment in 1898 of the Moscow Art Theatre, dedicated to the plays of Anton Chekhov (1860–1904). One of the founders of the MAT, Constantin Stanislavsky, quickly developed acting and staging techniques to make Chekhov's plays seem more real and more natural than anything seen in the theatre before.

Naturalism thus conquered the older nineteenth-century theatre of illusionism. The Moscow Art Theatre merely brought to perfection certain revolutionary developments already challenging the older styles and traditions and paved the way for the triumph of realism. Yeats, it has to be said, was somewhat dismayed by this victory and did not in fact accept it. At the Abbey he fought to maintain a theatre movement which had two strands: poetic drama (mainly written by himself) and realistic 'peasant plays' (best written by J. M. Synge) which owed a lot to the new naturalistic ideas on authenticity of setting, costume and acting style.

As time went on, the realistic side of the Abbey repertory seemed to win out over the poetic or symbolic. And yet it could be said that the Abbey plays, such as Synge's *Riders to the Sea* (1903) or Lady Gregory's *Spreading the News* (1904), were not realistic in the same way as, for example, Shaw's *Candida* (1895) or *Major Barbara* (1906). The Abbey plays usually had a remote, other-worldly flavour and did not seem directly to relate to the events and problems of contemporary life. After the premature death of Synge in 1909, however, others began to write more sordid, more genuinely realistic plays. Writers such as Lennox Robinson (1886–1958) and T. C. Murray (1873–1959) held the mirror up to disillusioned Irish life in the style of Ibsen's problem plays. Yeats, having abandoned the Abbey for the moment in order to write poetic plays modelled on the Japanese Noh drama in London, seemed about to give up the fight against realism in Dublin. He wrote a famous open letter to Lady Gregory in 1919: 'We did not set out to create this sort of theatre, and its success has been to me a discouragement and a defeat.' And yet, if Yeats could have been fair about this point, Abbey realism had already created some of the most striking and original work in the modern theatre, and was about to recreate former glories in the new drama of Sean O'Casey.

The second impulse was nationalism. Here the Abbey Theatre was quite unlike any other of the new little theatres in London, Paris, Berlin or Moscow, all of which concentrated on fighting the existing commercial theatres with a new set of artistic principles. The new Irish theatre complicated matters by making its foundation part of the movement in cultural nationalism which thrived in Dublin and elsewhere in Ireland from the early 1890s. The literary renaissance which then developed, headed by Yeats, celebrated independence as the goal worth fighting for. Home Rule seemed a real possibility as time went on, but there was a group of militant republicans (of whom Maud Gonne, Yeats's lover, was one) whose extremism penetrated all activities. These nationalists assumed that the Abbey Theatre, which was built on their support, had a duty to idealise Ireland first and be entertaining or satirical only when the consciousness-raising was accomplished. Therefore, when Synge began to write comedies which, far from idealising Ireland or Irish manners, actually held them up to some ridicule, the nationalist critics and supporters turned on 'their' theatre and demanded Synge's head. Yeats was determined to fight for artistic freedom, even where the artist took it upon him or herself to laugh at flaws and absurdities in Irish life. He answered the journalist and founder of Sinn Féin Arthur Griffith in 1905 by insisting that Synge had heard the story of *The*

Shadow of the Glen (1903) on the Aran Islands and not in Paris as Griffith, accusing Synge of French decadence, had said in his newspaper. Yeats was clearly arguing that Synge was being faithful to what he saw and heard among the people, and, according to Yeats's own definition in 'First Principles' (1904), national literature 'is the work of writers who are moulded by influences that are moulding their country, and who write out of so deep a life that they are accepted there in the end'. Synge's case was to be O'Casey's later on.

But first came the storm over Synge's *The Playboy of the Western World* in January 1907, which uncannily anticipated the riots that greeted *The Plough and the Stars* in February 1926. Synge's play, a comedy and a satire, greatly angered that section of the Abbey's audience who were either strong nationalists or members of the urban Catholic middle class, who resented this slur, as they saw it, on Irish rural people. In a programme note, Synge claimed once again that his play was based on reality ('suggested by an actual occurrence in the West') and that the language was also derived from the speech of the people. In short, he claimed *The Playboy* was realism. But its first audience took exception to what they saw and heard on patriotic grounds; in painting the people as fools, worshippers of a murderer, and (worst of all) immoral, this play *must* be a sneer at the 'real' Irish. Lady Gregory and Synge had to send a telegram to Yeats, who was lecturing in Scotland: 'Audience broke up in disorder at the word shift.' The reference was to Christy Mahon's speech, 'It's Pegeen I'm seeking only, and what'd I care if you brought me a drift of chosen females, standing in their shifts [underwear] itself, maybe, from this place to the eastern world?' The police were called in the next night, and the play went on amid uproar, the actors playing 'almost entirely in dumb show'. When Yeats returned on the next day he took over and determined to fight back in defence of artistic freedom. That night the police were there again, and many arrests were made. Yeats shouted at the audience his determination that *The Playboy* would not be taken off. And so it went, night after night, with up to fifty policemen in the aisles of the Abbey and opposition continuing. The play completed its short run and then Yeats arranged a public debate at the Abbey – to which Synge himself did not come. Yeats made one of his bravest speeches to a hostile audience; when they refused to listen he reminded them that he was the author of the patriotic play *Cathleen Ni Houlihan*.

The story of the *Playboy* riots makes clear the principles on which the Abbey was run. As a modern theatre, established as an alternative to commercialism, it was dedicated to forms of entertainment which were fundamentally artistic and truth-telling. As a theatre founded in the midst of a nationalist movement it was supposed to hold a mirror to the realities of Irish experience and of Irish history. But above all it stood for the writer: the Abbey was primarily a writers' theatre and an actors' theatre after that. And the writer had to be free to cultivate his or her vision of Ireland, regardless of propaganda.

O'Casey ran into exactly the same problems at the Abbey as Synge. However, it has to be said that O'Casey was more politicised. When he wrote *The Story of the Irish Citizen Army* (1919), an account of how Larkin's army formed, O'Casey had become somewhat disillusioned with Irish nationalism. But from the sidelines, as it were, he observed and continued to observe the factions which, after 1916, gradually united under the Sinn Féin umbrella and left Labour in the lurch. The flag of the ICA was the 'starry plough', representing the labourers toiling to reach the stars (i.e., some kind of spiritual fulfilment built upon their manual labour). To O'Casey, the 'plough and the stars' represented a struggle which should have been directed solely at the improvement of the workers' conditions. Hence his impatience with the blood-sacrifice of 1916. O'Casey further argued that after 1918 Irish Labour 'will probably have to fight Sinn Féin . . . but the labour leaders must become wiser and more broadminded than they at present seem to be' if they were to democratise the national movement.

Beginning with *The Shadow of a Gunman* (1923), O'Casey introduced a new form of realism to the Abbey Theatre. Because he could not afford the price of admission, he had been to the Abbey only twice before his own plays were staged there. One of the plays he saw was *Blight* (1918), a little-known drama by Oliver St John Gogarty which for the first time introduced the Dublin slums on to the stage. Here poverty, consumption and appalling living conditions 'blight' the lives of the ordinary Dublin characters. O'Casey's outlook was never so bleak or pessimistic, and he was always eager to contextualise his representations politically: that is, to locate his stories of tenement life within the political events and atmosphere of the day. This concern lent to O'Casey's plays their special distinction. Each play juxtaposes two worlds, the private and the public. The private is the life of the tenement dwellers, where indeed privacy is hardly to be thought of; and yet the families who encroach freely on each other's space are preoccupied with personal and domestic problems. The public life in O'Casey's plays inevitably means the political: he shows how the affairs of state and the ambitions of freedom hold the lives of ordinary people in a vice. There is no escape from the battles raging in the streets. There is no hiding place from the consequences of a movement dedicated to overthrowing the oppressor. O'Casey's point of view is neither nationalist nor unionist: on balance it is anti-unionist and anti-imperialist, but it is the 'balance' which matters. Compassion takes precedence over political allegiance or ideology; each of the three Dublin plays is called a 'tragedy'.

The laws of tragedy insist that pity and terror rather than political ideas should be primary. O'Casey's great achievement was to rise above local allegiances and turn the harsh conditions of working-class life into the materials of modern art.

It was stated above that the Abbey Theatre was and remains a writers' theatre first and an actors' second. Yet this is not to deny the contribution of the Abbey actors to the playwrights' achievements. From the beginning, the Abbey actors avoided the 'star system' dominant in the English and French theatres (whereby a production was mainly if not solely for the performances of some major actor or actress, while all other performers were supposed to keep out of the 'limelight' and subordinate their talents to the star's). The Abbey style is based on the ensemble, which means that no one individual gets top billing; all actors are regarded as equal. The actor playing a major role one night could well be in a minor role the next night (for the repertory system means a rapid change of plays). Further, the Abbey style is based on realism. The speech, gestures, movements and costume are all rooted in local conditions. In contrast to the English and French theatres of the early twentieth century, where 'received pronunciation' and a classical acting style dominated (and were supported by such training centres as the Royal Academy of Dramatic Art (RADA), the Oxford University Dramatic Society (OUDS), and the Comédie Française), the Abbey Theatre relied on the natural, inherent qualities of the performers. Authenticity took precedence over standardised elocution; the dominant value was 'peasant quality', or truth to native Irish experience.

At the time O'Casey's plays were first performed, an excellent company was in residence at the Abbey. It included the great F. J. McCormick (real name, Peter Judge), Barry Fitzgerald (real name, Will Shields), Sara Allgood, Maureen Delaney, Michael J. Dolan and Gabriel Fallon.

The same group of players acted in all of O'Casey's plays written for the Abbey, grew to know his work as intimately as the players at the Moscow Art Theatre knew their Chekhov, and as a result provided performances so convincing that audiences saw them as real. When *Juno* and *The Plough* transferred to London, only some of the original cast were included in the new productions, yet the playing of these original cast-members was recognised in London as startlingly original. The young Laurence Olivier, for example, was bowled over by the performances and vowed one day to play in *Juno*: he directed an outstanding production many years later (1966) at the National Theatre in London. In short, the Abbey players contributed enormously to the success of the plays on stage.

A final point refers to the staging. The original Abbey Theatre, which was destroyed by fire in 1951, was a small space with a capacity of just over 500 people. The stage was disproportionately small (curtain-line to back wall 16 feet 4 inches, proscenium opening 21 feet, width of stage wall-to-wall 40 feet). These dimensions, coupled with the absence of 'flies' or overhead space, meant that the staging had to be simple. Scenery was functional and unspectacular. Simplicity was the essence of every production. It is important to bear this point in mind because it means – as in the Elizabethan theatre – that a great deal of responsibility was thrown on language to create atmosphere, colour, variety and sheer entertainment. O'Casey's plays were sometimes termed 'Elizabethan' in style (usually by critics in London or New York) and this, basically, is the reason behind it. It is not that O'Casey was trying to be Shakespearean; it is that the theatre conditions required it. (Synge as well as O'Casey wrote poetic prose virtually to compensate for the lack of mise en-scène.) In reading O'Casey's plays, then, it is important not to think the language stilted or artificial but to imagine instead performances where language becomes a major resource which the characters, impoverished though they are, can exploit as a weapon, a defence against deprivation, and a source of rhetorical delight – a kind of richness – even for the poorest of the poor. Thus a new kind of poetry was invented for the modern stage.

REFERENCES

Greene, David and Edward M. Stephens, *J. M. Synge 1871–1909*, New York: Macmillan, 1959.

O'Casey, Sean, *The Story of the Irish Citizen Army* [1919], in *Feathers from the Green Crow: Sean O'Casey, 1905–1925*, ed. Robert Hogan, Columbia: University of Missouri Press, 1962.

Robinson, Lennox, *The History of the Abbey Theatre 1899–1951*, London: Sidgwick and Jackson, 1951.

Yeats, W. B., 'First Principles (1904)', in *Explorations*, London: Macmillan, 1961.

Introduction to
The Plough and the Stars

Without a doubt, *The Plough and the Stars* is O'Casey's greatest play. It is the one with the greatest intensity, the one which most ambitiously addresses the human comedy at the point where violent public events suddenly transform it into tragedy. It is the O'Casey play which tackles the greatest Irish theme, the fight for freedom, and humanises it with searing irony to equal the greatest critiques of war and peace to be found in literature, from Shakespeare's *Henry IV* to Bertolt Brecht's *Mother Courage and Her Children*.

The Plough and the Stars was intended as a critique of the 1916 Rising, ten years on. By this time, the new Free State had got under way but in various elections the cause of Labour fell more and more behind. To one of O'Casey's socialist persuasion this signalled a betrayal of the workers' cause which he and Jim Larkin had striven to protect from 1913. When Jim Larkin returned from prison in the United States (where he had been sentenced as an 'anarchist' for preaching socialism) in 1923 he tried to regain control over the Irish trade-union movement and instead felt the full resistance of the new men, comfortable in their secure, non-militant organisation. Larkin was made to feel a total outsider, was charged with embezzling union funds years earlier, and had to create for himself a rival trade-union organisation in the late 1920s. All of this confirmed for the embittered O'Casey that the new state was founded on bourgeois and not Labour principles. Looking back, he saw that the 1916 Rising was the clue to the problem.

This rebellion, undertaken through an alliance between James Connolly (who replaced Larkin as leader of the trade-union movement and chief of the Irish Citizen Army when Larkin went to America in 1914) and Pádraic Pearse, a teacher, a poet, a devotee of the Irish language and a prominent officer in the Irish Volunteers, was a total disaster. It took place in confusion, since Pearse and his supporters acted in defiance of higher orders to cancel the rebellion, orders that were in all the Sunday newspapers the day before the planned action, Easter Monday 1916. The Rising was thus a minor affair, confined to Dublin, and involved some 1,600 Volunteers and 300 members of the Irish Citizen Army. Pearse was the commander-in-chief, and he it was who read the proclamation of the Irish republic outside the General Post Office. By Saturday of Easter week all was over and Pearse surrendered. He and fourteen other leaders (including Connolly) were put on trial for treason and executed in Kilmainham jail in Dublin. They were quickly turned into martyrs by a population which had at first ridiculed the insurgents (the looting of shops in O'Connell Street which O'Casey depicts in *The Plough and the Stars* actually occurred, signifying the indifference of the poor people of Dublin to the lofty ideals proclaimed by Pearse across the street at the General Post Office). As the poet Yeats discerned (in 'Easter 1916'), all was changed, changed utterly by the executions and 'a terrible beauty was born'. As O'Casey read the situation, however, the 1916 Rising was the root of a succession of wars and acts of terror succeeded by the civil war of 1922–3, when those who had accepted the Treaty were opposed by those who saw it as a betrayal of 1916.

In O'Casey's analysis, the nationalist ideal was both romantic and dangerous. Labour's alliance with nationalism was, in his view, a tragic mistake which abandoned the cause of the poor and the unemployed. He was thus prepared to pour scorn on the whole 1916 endeavour as fatally misguided. Its representation onstage was to shock audiences ill-prepared for this kind of satire.

On the fourth night of its first production at the Abbey Theatre, in February 1926, *The Plough* was greeted by riots of a similar kind to those which had greeted Synge's masterpiece *The Playboy of the Western World* in January 1907. The reception of O'Casey's masterpiece, accordingly, marked a crisis in the modern Irish theatre. Violent opposition to a playwright's vision threatens the very foundation on which art makes its stand, namely the free expression of individual feeling. O'Casey's vision resembled Synge's in this: both were satirists of pretence and hypocrisy. But O'Casey's point of view was far more political than Synge's and so the offence he caused to a section of the audience arose from his deliberate repudiation of nationalism whereas Synge, as W. B. Yeats memorably recorded, 'was unfitted to think a political thought'.

Since the circumstances of the opposition at the Abbey Theatre throw some light on the play itself it may be worthwhile to provide a few details here. The problem began with the second act, where the prostitute Rosie Redmond sets the scene in the public house. This was a shocking innovation in itself, and clearly O'Casey intended to bring together in a spirit of mockery patriotism (outside the public house) and prostitution (within). When a member of the Abbey Board had objected to the character of Rosie some months before the production, Yeats himself was firm in her defence: 'She is certainly as necessary to the general action and idea as are the drunkards and wastrels. O'Casey is contrasting the ideal dream [that is, the patriotic dream expressed by the Figure in the Window] with the normal grossness of life, and of that she [Rosie] is an essential part' (Lady Gregory, *Journals*). To his credit, Yeats insisted on Rosie's being left in the script. O'Casey's satire made itself felt on the audience as Act

Two progressed: the words of Pádraic Pearse used by the Figure in the Window were recognised, and the contrast between their high-mindedness and the low life and vulgarity of the working-class characters in the pub became increasingly obvious. The climax came when the three men in uniform, Clitheroe, Langon and Brennan, entered carrying the two flags of the combatant Irish forces, the tricolour of the National Volunteers and the plough-and-stars of the Irish Citizen Army. It happened that on the fourth night of the production there was present a large number of women closely associated with the 'men of 1916', those who had fought, died, or had been imprisoned. The sight of the flags sparked off massive resistance to what was perceived as an insult to the patriot dead. 'Women screamed and sang songs . . . A red-haired damsel in the gallery removed her shoes and flung them heatedly into the mêlée beneath.' Then the fight began in earnest:

> Twenty women rushed from the pit to the stalls. Two of them succeeded in reaching the stage, where a general mêlée took place. The invading women were thrown bodily back into the orchestra. A young man then tried to reach the stage, but was cut off by the lowering of the curtain. This he grabbed, swinging out on it in a frantic endeavour to pull it down. Women rushed to aid him in this project, but he was suddenly thrown into the stalls by a sharp blow from one of the actors. The pandemonium created a panic among a section of the audience, who dashed for the exits and added to the confusion.
>
> As soon as the curtain was raised again, up dashed another youth to the stage and got into grips with two actresses opening the next scene. Immediately a couple of actors rushed from the wings and unceremoniously pushed off the intruder. Another man had got on the

stage by this time and was attacked by a number of players. He retaliated vigorously, and after several blows were exchanged, a hardy punch on the jaw [by Barry Fitzgerald] hurled him into the stalls.

Meanwhile altercations were going on among the two sections of the audience. For several minutes the players calmly walked up and down the stage, but the performance was not resumed. A change came over the troubled scene when a party of detectives and uni-formed police arrived and quickly distributed them-selves through different parts of the house . . .

(Lowery, *Whirlwind*, pp. 30–31)

Yeats then came forward to address the audience. Now at the height of his powers and loaded with honours (the Nobel Prize had been awarded him in 1923), Yeats spoke with great authority. He was a Senator in the upper house of the Irish Free State government; he was chairman of the Abbey's Board of Directors and its managing director; he was not only the voice of the Abbey Theatre but virtually the voice of liberated Ireland. And what he had to say was to recall the days of Synge's reception over *The Playboy of the Western World* and to rebuke the present audience: 'You have disgraced yourselves again. Is this to be an ever-recurring celebration of the arrival of Irish genius? Once more you have rocked the cradle of genius.' O'Casey's repu-tation was established, he said, through this negative and violent response. 'This is his apotheosis.' (Lowery, p. 31).

O'Casey had to look up 'apotheosis' in his dictionary when he got home. To his surprise, he found that Yeats had placed him among the gods. Yet O'Casey knew all too well that to many people he was in the gutter, having betrayed the ideals of the 1916 Rising. As he left the theatre that night O'Casey was verbally abused by a group of nationalist women, who called him a traitor and a pro-Britain propagandist. ' "Yes," said one, leaning against the wall, "an' I'd like you to know that there isn't a prostitute in Ireland from one end of it to th' other." ' (*Inishfallen, Fare Thee Well*, pp. 176–7).

A public debate followed, first in the newspapers and then in a hall rented for the occasion on 1 March 1926. O'Casey's main opponent was Mrs Hannah Sheehy-Skeffington, a suffragette and widow of the pacifist shot by a British soldier during Easter Week, 1916. She was a woman of considerable presence, who spoke on behalf of all women involved in the 1916 Rising, and she had much support at the debate. Her main point was that *The Plough and the Stars* was 'a travesty of Easter Week, and that it concentrated on pettiness and squalor, unrelieved by a gleam of heroism' (Lowery, p. 100). O'Casey replied as best he could, saying he had not tried to write about 'heroes' and never would. Maud Gonne McBride, once Yeats's beloved, made the point that if O'Casey did not believe in heroes he should not have introduced a real one into his play in the form of Pádraic Pearse.

The issue was thus quite clear-cut: to the republicans and especially the women in that camp, *The Plough* was a disgraceful slur on those who had fought and died in 1916 and on that basis alone ought to be swept from the stage of the so-called national theatre. To O'Casey himself and his supporters, *The Plough* was great art and on this basis should be acclaimed, regardless of political considerations. Here was a play, however, where the art-versus-politics argument could never be resolved. *The Plough* is a political play; it is a modern history play. It is also a humanist play, in which characters and their fates appeal very strongly to audiences' feelings. The conflict between ideology and artistic achievement was and remains the major critical question surrounding *The Plough and the Stars*.

For O'Casey himself, the row over *The Plough* had life-long implications. His *Juno and the Paycock* had been playing successfully in a London theatre since November

1925 and he was now invited over to supervise its transfer to a bigger theatre in March 1926. This would mark a major break with Dublin and the working-class conditions which had formed O'Casey as man and writer. He was aware what a big step it was, though at first he thought it would be temporary. He left Dublin on 5 March 1926 and was never again to return to live in Ireland. Thus *The Plough and the Stars*, which was to become an international success in due course, and the play most often revived at the Abbey Theatre, by its first reception brought to an end an important phase in O'Casey's career. His next play, *The Silver Tassie* (1928), would be rejected by the Abbey and would cause another great controversy. O'Casey settled in England and never again wrote for the Abbey Theatre. Thereby he lost a workshop and a body of actors to write for and to collaborate with. His exile was, in a way, tragic.

REFERENCES

Gregory, Lady Augusta, *Lady Gregory's Journals, Vol. 2, Books 30–44*, ed. Daniel J. Murphy, Gerrards Cross: Colin Smythe, 1987, 20 Sept. 1925, pp. 41, 42.

Lowery, Robert, ed., *A Whirlwind in Dublin: 'The Plough and the Stars' Riots*, Westport, CT: Greenwood Press, 1984, pp. 30–31, 100.

O'Casey, Sean, *Inishfallen, Fare Thee Well: Autobiography, Book 4: 1917–1926*, London: Pan Books, 1972, pp. 176–7.

Structure and Action

It should be obvious, after reading the play, that *The Plough and the Stars* is not structured along conventional lines. A well-made play would have developed from an opening situation into a domestic crisis, then into complications with various threats to happiness, until the 'obligatory scene' was reached and the expected confrontation took place, leaving only the dénouement of the plot to take place in the closing scene. In *The Plough and the Stars* there is no single plot as such. True, we join the young Clitheroe couple in the opening scenes and form the impression that the play will deal with their love and fortunes in the face of imminent political crisis. But O'Casey did not write in this way. *The Plough and the Stars* is actually more extreme in its avoidance of conventional dramatic form than either of O'Casey's previous plays (*The Shadow of a Gunman* and *Juno and the Paycock*).

Act Two, in fact, is the key to the structure because, even though he avoided the form of the well-made play, O'Casey, as artist, had to provide the form which would best accommodate the content of his play. Act Two was originally a one-act play entitled *The Cooing of Doves*, submitted to the Abbey in the early 1920s and rejected. When he began to write *The Plough* in October 1924, then entitled *The Easter Lily Aflame*, what was in O'Casey's mind, he says, was that he had already written a play about the 'Black-and-Tan period' (1920) and a play about the Irish civil war (1922–3), 'but no play yet around the period of the actual Easter Rising, which was the beginning of all that happened afterward' (Ayling, *Casebook*, p. 139). So that became his theme, and he allowed it to grow and combine in his mind with such symbols as the Irish flag, the tricolour, and the flag of the Irish Citizen Army, the plough-and-stars. 'I never make a scenario [plot outline], depending on the natural growth of a play rather than on any method of joinery' (Ayling, Casebook, p. 140). He brings the two flags together in a public house, while outside the meeting takes place, corresponding to the actual meeting on 25 October 1915 which reconciled the Volunteers (under Pádraic Pearse) and the Irish Citizen Army (under James Connolly). In particular, the flag of the Irish Citizen Army, symbolising the workers ever aspiring to higher things, gave O'Casey his theme. 'It was this flag that fired in my mind the title for the play; and the events that swirled around the banner and that of the Irish Volunteers . . . that gave me all the humour, pathos and dialogue that fill the play' (Ayling, *Casebook*, p. 139). The structure thus grew from a central idea: the betrayal of the cause of Labour by the delusion of romantic patriotism. (This betrayal was even more clear when Labour failed to gain support in elections following the foundation of the Irish Free State in 1922.) Because of this thematic approach, the play does not suffer when Nora Clitheroe and her family problems are left out of Act Two. That act, O'Casey tells us, was filled largely by the rejected *The Cooing of Doves*: 'It went in with but a few minor changes' (Ayling, *Casebook*, p. 140).

The key to Act Two, and thus the key to the structure of *The Plough* as a whole, lies in the juxtaposition of two totally contrasting worlds of experience. This is how O'Casey as playwright usually got his best effects. In this instance, the outside world of high-minded politics, articulated by the Figure in the Window, is violently brought into contact with the inside world of ordinary people satisfying basic human appetites. This collision releases a powerful delivery of irony. It is not that O'Casey mocks the speeches of the Figure in the Window: it is worth noting how the people in the pub often praise his words and respond with enthusiasm ('It's th' sacred thruth, mind you, what that man's afther sayin',' p. 35). The real point is that this enthusiasm is a form of intoxication, or, looked at the other way, the pub is a metaphor for the political response of the working class to idealistic rhetoric.

When the fighting begins in the pub, first between Mrs Gogan and Mrs Burgess and then between the Covey and Fluther, we have to see these battles as something of a parody of the great fight for freedom being eulogised by the Figure in the Window. Thus, the juxtaposition of high and low ideals is comic and provides the structural means for O'Casey to expose the dangerous inadequacy of the Figure's language and doctrine.

After Act Two the action returns to the domestic concerns of Nora Clitheroe and from this point to the end what we witness is tragic displacement. As the Rising breaks out and Nora goes in search of her husband Jack, the contrast is heightened between two sets of values, the domestic and the militaristic. The domestic values include fertility, the bringing of new life, as in Nora's pregnancy; the militaristic values include bloodshed, the destruction of life, as in Lieutenant Langon's wounds and the corpse that Nora describes, where 'every twist of his body was a cry against th' terrible thing that had happened to him' (p. 61). If we are reading the play adequately we will notice that Nora's pregnancy/fertility carries forward the motif of Mrs Gogan's baby in Act Two, embroiled in a battle that is comic there but deadly serious in Act Three. Nora's premature baby joins Mollser in the coffin in Act Four, underlining the waste and needlessness of such infant mortality.

O'Casey's way of organising the action, then, is to run several little plots at once, overlapping and repeating themes and motifs, and through these parallels and contrasts moving the main action along, which is the ill-fated attempt by Nora to keep her family together and to expand it.

In this pattern of repetitive action the use of space should be noticed. In complete defiance of the common description of his dramatic art as realistic, O'Casey increasingly used symbolism and other anti-realistic forms. The pub in Act Two and how it is combined with the exterior scene of the political meeting has already been commented on. The space onstage is in this way used in a style one would have to call *expressionistic*: that is, the Figure in the Window (who remains unnamed) looms up as if from a dream and invades the space of the public house with his voice and blurry presence. This is not realism, but a more experimental and more effective mode of staging the action.

Act Three, indeed, transfers to the streets, and the space provides an image of people very much 'on the outside', powerless, removed from both the fight for freedom (which does not concern them) and from any share in the material wealth of society. When the Woman from Rathmines briefly enters this space we see vividly, if briefly, what a dead end, what a vacuum, it is: she desperately needs to escape to the safety of her middle-class suburb. By this time the looting has started, and the deprived people's need to steal in order to have a lifestyle equal to the middle class is vividly seen in Mrs Gogan and Mrs Burgess allying to bring home consumer goods of all kinds. A carnival spirit contrasts sharply with the background of the Rising, and O'Casey's Elizabethan style of staging allows these two actions to go on at the same time without a change of scene: the entrance of the three soldiers, with Langon badly wounded, underlines the success of this staging method here.

Then Act Four brings us to Bessie Burgess's dingy flat at the top of the tenement. Here, the symbolism is all too apparent: the apartment has '*a look of compressed confinement*' (p. 78). The space symbolises a trap, '*poverty bordering on destitution*'. It is the end of the line. Here

Nora is displaced, out of her element, out of her home, and out of her mind. The setting allows this tragic stage of the action sharp definition. The coffin onstage in such a confined space, which the men use as a card-table, is a powerful image. It is waiting to be taken out; so too are the men; the surprise is that Bessie is also to be removed, dead, and the space finally occupied by the two British soldiers. The outside world of militarism thus finally invades and takes over the inside world of domestic safety, and the action is complete. The setting, the staging, the image of the soldiers sitting to drink the tea Nora made for Jack and their joining in the song outside, provide a masterly unification of theme and action. We see here, if we haven't seen it already, how O'Casey weaves together the various strands of the action so that there is finally created a devastating and ironic effect. This converging on the final image of the fire within, the fire without, the song without matched by the song within, concentrates the viewer's or reader's response in such a way that she or he is moved by the tragic destruction, the pincer movement of events, which has befallen the helpless residents of this symbolic tenement house.

REFERENCE

Ayling, Ronald, ed., *O'Casey: The Dublin Trilogy: A Casebook*, London: Macmillan, 1985, pp. 171–87.

Characters and Themes

By the time he came to write *The Plough and the Stars* O'Casey well understood the primacy of characterisation in drama. This is not to deny the importance of 'action', but it is to declare quite emphatically that O'Casey's plays are not plot-driven but character-driven. Technically, what O'Casey does breaks the rules of good dramaturgy – a playwright isn't supposed to introduce a character once only and never even have her mentioned by another character: witness Rosie Redmond, seen only in Act Two. A more glaring example is the unnamed Woman from Rathmines, who has no more than one page of text in Act Three and is never seen or heard of again. Even O'Casey himself, a stout defender of his experimental style, later condemned this episode. The Woman, he wrote in *The Green Crow* (1956), 'had neither rhyme nor reason for being there; a character that was in every way a false introduction; one who could have no conceivable connection with any of the others from the play's beginning to the play's end' (p. 9). But this character is not usually omitted in production because, like Rosie Redmond, she throws light on the realities of Irish life in the period in which *The Plough* is set. The Woman from Rathmines is an extreme case, but her inclusion indicates how O'Casey understood characterisation. In general, his characters exist to show something rather than to do something: we see what they stand for, not in the sense that we see immediately that Rosie Redmond is a prostitute but in the sense that she is dependent on men, that she is exploited by her landlord, that she is one of the defenceless whom the Rising will ignore and fail to help.

Characters in O'Casey do not do much; they are not agents of action in the conventional dramatic sense. Like characters in Dickens's novels or in some comic parts of Shakespeare's history plays (because O'Casey's Dublin plays are really history plays), O'Casey's characters are on the margins of great events rather than in the thick of them. What we see is how they cope with their power-lessness. Usually, they cope by inventing and sustaining eccentricities of manner and speech which force others in the community to beware and to make space for them. Once given that space – and a character like Peter Flynn is perpetually complaining that he is not given this space – an O'Casey character will settle into a performance of the invented role rather than actually do anything which changes the situation.

Therefore, in *The Plough and the Stars* for the most part one has characters who jostle for the space in which to perform the role that brings each of them compensation for loss of social and economic status. Thus Mrs Gogan, for example, whose voice is the first one we hear in the play, is a widow with many children to support, one of whom is the dying Mollser and another a baby, and yet Mrs Gogan is a curious, busy-body type who takes pleasure in the spectacle of death. There is, of course, something comical about this macabre side of Mrs Gogan, but the point to be made is *her need to avoid the realities of her own economic position*. She invents things: she decides that the delivery of Nora's hat is a sign of Nora's snobbery. But we soon learn that the hat is a present from Jack and so is not a sign of Nora's self-indulgence at all. When it comes to Mollser's consumption, because there is nothing she can do for her, Mrs Gogan prefers to believe Mollser is getting better. When she is told at one point that Mollser 'looks as if she was goin' to faint', she is quick to snap back, 'She's never any other way but faintin'!' (p. 70). Mrs Gogan fights with Bessie Burgess for the perambulator only to use it for looting: this is the only action she takes and it is a significant one. Rising or no Rising, she has to feed and clothe her family and will steal to do so. She is finally 'in her element' when Mollser dies, as Fluther notes: 'mixin' earth to earth, an' ashes t'ashes an' dust to dust, an' revellin' in plumes an' hearses, last days an' judgements!' (p. 87). This 'performance' element is a part of her character.

It is also a part of the characters of Uncle Peter and the Covey. Each of these is a caricature or two-dimensional type, exaggerated for amusement. Each exists mainly – like characters out of Dickens – to maintain endlessly the provocative and/or irritable responses they show from the very outset. One would have to say, however, that the Covey, for all that he is a caricature of a swaggering know-all, is to some extent O'Casey's spokesman on the political meaning of the play. One can instance three occasions where this is so:

(1) In Act One the Covey accuses the Irish Citizen Army of bringing disgrace to the flag, the plough-and-stars, because it was a Labour flag and ought not to be associated with a middle-class nationalist revolution such as the Volunteers were planning.

(2) When the Figure in the Window (Act Two) praises war as a glorious thing, which had already brought 'heroism' back to Europe in World War I and which must be welcomed in Ireland as the 'Angel of God', the Covey dismisses this idea as mere 'dope' (p. 43). He goes on to repeat this charge to Fluther (p. 48), and a row develops. Whereas the Covey is a troublemaker, and is satirised as a socialist fanatic, O'Casey actually shared the Covey's belief about Pearse's speech. Therefore, the Covey is useful in the play as a counterblast to Pearse's romantic nationalism.

(3) In the last act, when the Covey preaches to the English soldier about the evils of consumption arising from the capitalist system, Corporal Stoddart concedes

the point and adds that he is a socialist himself but has to do his duty as a soldier nevertheless. The Covey argues that the only duty of a socialist is the emancipation of the workers, and when Stoddart replies that one has to fight for his country just the same we get the telling question from Fluther: 'You're not fightin' for your counthry here, are you?' (p. 88), thus pointing up the false analysis made by this confused Englishman, whose nationalism, like the nationalism of the Irish Volunteers, has taken precedence over socialism and has left problems like consumption unsolved.

The Covey is therefore responsible for injecting into the play the major *agon* or debating point on which the tragedy depends, for O'Casey's own analysis was that the 1916 Rising was a mistake so far as the Dublin working class was concerned. The Clitheroes, standing for that class, are destroyed because of the nationalism to which Jack Clitheroe gives service (and his life). It is ironic that the irritating Covey, who is an armchair socialist and a bore, should nevertheless be the one to point up the flaw in the ideology driving the combatants.

O'Casey's representation of Jack Clitheroe differs from his more detailed characterisation of Nora, Fluther and Bessie, the three main characters in *The Plough*. It is obvious from the outset that Clitheroe's involvement in the fight for freedom is governed more by personal vanity than by political principle; both Mrs Gogan and Nora herself comment on his vanity. When Clitheroe switches from amorous stay-at-home to stern authoritarian in Act One it is only because his promotion in the Irish Citizen Army was kept secret by Nora. When he enters in Act Three in the midst of the Rising, the first thing Clitheroe says to Nora is that he wishes he had never left her (p. 72). Just as Bernard Shaw revealed the harsh realities of battle through the professional soldier Bluntschli in *Arms and the Man* (1894), so O'Casey exposes the frightening realities of revolution through the experience of Clitheroe. To this extent O'Casey's theme and purpose are pacifist. He brings out this theme much more fully in his characterisation of Nora. Meanwhile, Clitheroe is shown caught up in a romantic battle fuelled first by fanaticism and then by fear. His character disappears under the rubble of the Imperial Hotel, whose destruction Brennan graphically describes in Act Four. Brennan tries to transform Clitheroe's terrible death into a heroic end, but as Bessie Burgess points out Clitheroe was simply abandoned in a burning building (p. 83). O'Casey's insistence on stripping Clitheroe of heroic status is a major part of his pacifist theme.

Nora Clitheroe is presented in a more complex way than Jack or any of the minor characters. In the best drama, characters are both admirable and the opposite; at times we sympathise and at other times we are repelled. On the one hand Nora is clearly ambitious, a woman with drive and energy who is determined to get out of the tenements as soon as she can build up the means; hence the two lodgers in a small apartment. She has aspiration to middle-class status: she talks much of 'respectability' in Act One as among her primary aims for the household. All of this angers Bessie Burgess and fills Mrs Gogan with contempt ('"Many a good one", says I, "was reared in a tenement house",' p. 7). Nora expresses one of the major themes in the play when she emphasises the importance of the home and the need both to protect it and help it to prosper. As the play opens Nora is employing Fluther to fix a lock on her door – a move which Bessie sees as an insult to her personally – and this is symbolic. Nora needs to shut out trouble from the home. Mollser admires Nora's abilities as home-maker and wonders if she herself will ever be strong enough 'to be keepin' a home together for a man' (p. 31). This purpose might strike us today as somewhat sexist but the representation of women as nurturers and home-makers is crucial to O'Casey's mode of thinking. It is a premise or a given of this play, in particular, that masculine and feminine values are sharply differentiated: war and destruction of life are here destructive of the home, fertility and new life.

Nora in this regard has a symbolic function. She stands for everything that is not death-bringing and is life-preserving. In Act Three we see clearly Nora's hatred of war as the agent of destruction of domestic life. Her passion makes her see only the fear and 'cowardice' of the combatants, 'afraid to say they're afraid' (p. 61). The women who opposed *The Plough* and who rioted on the fourth night saw Nora as the enemy, the spokesperson for O'Casey's anti-republicanism. But O'Casey deliberately allows Nora to become hysterical and to become excessive in her feelings against the Rising: this is her character, not O'Casey's propaganda. And he allows Mrs Gogan – of all people – to counter Nora's charge of the men's cowardice: 'Oh, they're not cowards anyway' (p. 61). We sympathise with Nora but we feel she goes 'over the top' in her reaction. Similarly, in Act Four, we are mainly sympathetic towards Nora in her broken state but we see, too, that she causes the death of Bessie Burgess. Nora's weakness creates tragic conflict. She chooses to chase out after Jack in the battle, which causes the miscarriage which in turn loses her her sanity; her best efforts fail to save Jack and that scenario is tragic by any definition. What we must conclude is that Nora is at times irritating and at times entirely sympathetic. Her humanity resides in this contradiction, and makes her all the more impressive as a dramatic creation.

The critic Ronald Ayling refers to O'Casey's skill in 'distancing' his major characters and this is what we find with Nora, Fluther and Bessie. They are not allowed to win our unqualified approval. On the contrary, for much of the play Fluther and Bessie are presented negatively. From the start Fluther is the common man: friendly, tolerant, amusing, but with a weakness for strong liquor. One of the first London critics of *The Plough*, James Agate, referred to Fluther as 'Falstaffian', and the description has stuck because of its aptness. Shakespeare's Falstaff is larger than life, robust, irresponsible, fond of drinking, Lord of Misrule, and not only witty in himself but the cause of wit in others. Fluther shows in Act Two how Falstaffian he can be, and is rewarded with Rosie Redmond's company as he leaves the pub. In the argument with the Covey, Fluther may not show intellectual superiority but he wins our hearts through his sheer unwillingness to be overcome by scientific jargon. In Act Three his Falstaffian nature is plainly on view when, ignoring the glorious cause which set his blood boiling in Act Two, he returns stone drunk from looting and cries out his defiance and indifference: 'Th' whole city can topple home to hell, for Fluther!' (p. 76). Finally, he fails Nora in her hour of need when he is incapable of going to fetch a doctor. He is thus anything but a hero; he is more the comic braggart thrown into a tragic situation. Thus we are 'distanced' and forced to see Fluther's faults alongside his attractions.

This 'distancing' method is combined with what Ronald Ayling calls O'Casey's 'balancing' of the dramatic action. There is no dominating character in *The Plough*, because O'Casey wanted always to present the group, the community, as the dramatic focus. Individual characters dominate for a scene or so and 'are then firmly distanced before they can disrupt the balance of the whole' (Ayling, p. 178). Thus Fluther – like Nora – is at times admired (for example, when he brings Nora safely home), and at other times blamed (as when he is too drunk to help further). In Act Four we see Fluther standing up bravely to the aggressive Sergeant (p. 93), and here the better side of his character is again on view. Yet this is the same Fluther who swallows down his looted whiskey as if there were no tomorrow: 'If I'm goin' to be whipped away, let me be whipped away when it's empty, an' not when it's half full!' (p. 81). Against that amusing self-indulgence we must place Mrs Gogan's tribute to Fluther's help with the funeral arrangement for Mollser (p. 89). He is thus a tissue of contradictory qualities, and in a strange way these contradictions make him seem more rather than less convincing.

Bessie Burgess is the greatest example of O'Casey's skill in characterisation in *The Plough*. Introduced as a termagant, Bessie is provided with a history which renders her political attitude as meaningful as her social aggression: she is presumably widowed – no Mr Burgess is ever mentioned, and from her rebuke to Mrs Gogan in Act Two about 'weddin' lines' (p. 44) it is likely there was a Mr Burgess – and she has a son fighting the Germans in Flanders and about to return home with a shattered arm (p. 90). Bessie stands out, then, as a loyalist, a Protestant unionist, in a community predominantly Roman Catholic and separatist. Her courage marks her out when she opposes the Easter Rising by flaunting the Union Jack from her window and singing 'Rule, Britannia' at the top of her voice (p. 60).

But courage aside, there is a marvellous wholeness about Bessie Burgess, a mixture of hostility and generosity, aggression and tenderness, cruelty and uncommon kindness. She confronts Nora for her air of superiority in Act One and Mrs Gogan for her breach of decorum in bringing a baby into a public bar among men. She is a fighter, literally in Act Two, verbally in Act Three (over the pram), and at most other times. But with Mollser she is kind and gentle: *'she gives a mug of milk to Mollser silently'* (p. 62). The 'silently' is typical. When Nora is in trouble towards the end of Act Three it is Bessie who first goes outside and carries her in, and then risks life and limb to go for a doctor in spite of her personal dislike of Nora – actions speak louder than words.

And, of course, in Act Four we see the extent of Bessie's charity and generosity when she mothers, nurses and protects the damaged Nora in her own cramped apartment. Bessie is killed trying to preserve Nora's life, and the Christian strength of her action is by no means undermined when Bessie reverts to her earlier scorn for Nora as she realises she has been shot on her account. Her use of the word 'bitch' here (p. 96) was rightly defended by Yeats as 'necessary' when the unofficial censor tried to remove it from the script: 'the scene is magnificent and we are loth to alter a word of it' (Lady Gregory, *Journals*). The word was retained. It is part of the proof that O'Casey's representation of Bessie was *not* sentimental but realistic.

In his portrayal of Bessie, then, O'Casey is careful once again to ensure that she remains ambivalent. As Ayling justly remarks (p. 186), 'We neither admire nor despise her indiscriminately, for her heroic stature is enhanced, though never exaggerated, by seeing her character in perspective.'

The ambivalences and contradictions O'Casey introduces into his characterisation in *The Plough* provide just the sort of distancing which allows the reader/spectator to see the play critically and to appreciate what Jack Lindsay (p. 193) calls its 'full dialectics' – that is, how the clashing ideologies within this society are seen in their irreconcilable conflict.

REFERENCES

Agate, James, 'The Plough and the Stars (1926)', in Sean O'Casey: Modern Judgements, ed. Ronald Ayling, London: Macmillan, 1969, pp. 79–81.

Ayling, Ronald, ed., O'Casey: The Dublin Trilogy: A Casebook, London: Macmillan, 1985, pp. 171–87.

Gregory, Lady Augusta, Lady Gregory's Journals, Vol. 2, Books 30–44, ed. Daniel J. Murphy, Gerrards Cross: Colin Smythe, 1987, 20 Sept. 1925, pp. 41, 42.

Lindsay, Jack, 'The Plough and the Stars Reconsidered', in The Sean O'Casey Review, 2.2 (1976), pp. 187–95.

Language

O'Casey's language is both realistic and poetic. Although this is a paradox it is probably the key to understanding O'Casey's procedures. On the one hand the Abbey tradition was predominantly realistic, using onstage the speech of the Irish people in all its regional and dialectical forms. A glance at P. W. Joyce's *English As We Speak It in Ireland* (1910) indicates what this means. English spoken in Ireland is historically inflected: as the language of the coloniser it retained a lot of words, phrases and pronunciation dating from the sixteenth to the eighteenth centuries. O'Casey's language records and elaborates Dublin speech.

The Plough exhibits a richness of speech in two quite different ways. One is through expansion of a statement for special effect beyond what is strictly necessary. An example is Nora's heated response in Act One to Jack's sexual advances: 'It's hard for a body to be always keepin' her mind bent on makin' thoughts that'll be no longer than th' length of your own satisfaction' (p. 26). This is a rather poetic way of saying, 'It's hard to say the right thing,' but Nora's way of putting it neatly turns realism aside in favour of alliteration (*m*ind . . . *m*akin' . . . *l*onger than th' *l*ength' . . .) and euphemism ('sexual satisfaction'). Another example is Fluther's advice to Mrs Gogan in Act Two to ignore Bessie Burgess: 'Th' safest way to hindher her from havin' any enjoyment out of her spite, is to *dip our thoughts into the fact of her bein' a female person* that has moved out of th' sight of ordinary sensible people' (p. 42, emphasis added). This simply means, 'It's best to ignore her completely', but the beauty of the speech lies in the adept cultivation of more words than are strictly

xliv

necessary. Looked at more closely, Fluther's speech uses a powerful metaphor ('to dip our thoughts'), but the metaphor keeps sliding into clauses that seem, but refuse, to clarify it ('the fact of her bein' a female person that . . .'). It is rhetoric which delights through its ornateness.

The language used in the play is often hyperbolic in this way: it uses excess for effect. Uncle Peter's language is piled high with unnecessary words which nevertheless provide a wonderful rhythm and sense of exaggeration: 'I'll leave you to th' day when th' all-pitiful, all-merciful, all-lovin' God 'll be handin' you to th' angels to be rievin' an' roastin' you, tearin' an' tormentin' you, burnin' an' blastin' you!' (p. 15). The sentence builds up to the word 'God', and seems a patient prayer, but then it turns around and calls for the 'angels', when Peter secretly means 'demons', to torture the Covey without mercy. The whole speech is a comic about-turn which reveals the vindictiveness of the hypocritical Peter. His use of alliteration within phrases coupling verbs of destruction (*t*earin' and *t*ormentin', etc.) provides delight to the audience.

Peter is not alone in being gifted with this ornate language. Virtually all of the characters within the tenements use this energetic speech as if it were their main resource in an economy which deprives them of real power. Peter curses eloquently simply because he can take no action. Language *is* power to these characters. Its power is sometimes comic, as when Fluther remarks, 'when you'd look at him [Peter], you'd wondher whether th' man was makin' fun o' th' costume, or th' costume was makin' fun o' th' man!' (p. 41). But the language is usually aggressive as well as comic. Indeed, the language is most often funny *because* the purpose is aggressive: these characters are nearly always verbally sparring, because they can't usefully engage in any action.

There is a second type of speech in *The Plough* and that is the more carefully constructed long speech. Here O'Casey was probably influenced by the use of the 'set speech' in Shakespeare. Because O'Casey's characters greatly admire language and frequently use it expertly to put down or displace others, it follows that they also admire a good speech themselves. This is part of the Irish tradition, found also, for example, in Synge's *The Playboy of the Western World*. Thus when the Figure in the Window begins his address – 'It is a glorious thing to see arms in the hands of Irishmen' (p. 34) – the response in the pub is immediate. Rosie describes the words as 'sacred thruth'; the Barman says if he was a little younger they would send him 'plungin' mad into th' middle of it!' (p. 35). Peter and Fluther are physically affected by the rhetoric, intoxicated by it even before they touch a drop of whiskey. Fluther describes the speeches as pattering on the people's heads like rain falling on corn, generative, stirring and productive. In short, the political rhetoric is *moving*. O'Casey lets these speeches from the Figure in the Window (all four of them) have their own effect: he does not put them into dialect spelling, and he does not suggest that they are in any way ironic. He allows them their formality, their high style, and he allows them their powerful effect.

This effect culminates in the strange, incantatory, religious language of the three soldiers who enter with the flags towards the end of Act Two. Having heard the Figure's speeches outside, they are stirred to die for Ireland. They agree that Ireland is greater than a mother and greater than a wife. Hearing now the final speech, an excerpt from Pádraic Pearse's oration over the grave of the Fenian hero O'Donovan Rossa, the three soldiers are in a state not just of fanaticism but of dangerous ecstasy as they pledge themselves to die for the independence of Ireland: 'So help us God!' (p. 53). The point is that the political rhetoric has aroused political madness. O'Casey establishes this point through equating language with intoxicating liquor. Nora's anti-war speeches in Act Three should be looked at as rhetoric answering the speeches of the Figure in the Window.

A different example of the longer speech is seen in the 'flyting match' in Act Three between Mrs Gogan and Bessie Burgess. A flyting match was a medieval debate which could become violent. We have a good example when Mrs Gogan and Bessie argue over who has more right to appropriate the pram (for the purposes of looting). Consider Mrs Gogan's speech which begins: 'That remark of yours, Mrs Bessie Burgess' (p. 67); the point she has to make is that the pram was left in her care. Mrs Burgess retaliates with the point that Mrs Gogan's complaints about the pram as an obstruction disqualify any claim she has to its use. Both speeches are metaphysical: they are plainly empty rhetoric. It is like the jargon used by negotiators in an industrial dispute: language as smokescreen for self-interest. The fact that the two women form an alliance and go out sharing the pram underlines the power of language once again. Each woman may have been speaking nonsense but having failed, like wrestlers, to gain a knockout, they agree on a draw and share the spoils. O'Casey uses this farcical moment to draw out the comic side of difference. In a parody of the alliance between the Volunteers and the Irish Citizen Army he shows how practical self-interest with a material end in view is far more meaningful to the deprived classes than theoretical debate. Language as a form of looting is gleefully celebrated.

A final and different example is what in classical drama is called the 'Nuntius's speech'. Towards the end of a tragedy a messenger usually enters to announce what has happened to Oedipus or Agamemnon or whoever, inside the palace. A long speech is delivered, full of details calculated to stir the hearts of the audience and prepare them for the final speeches of lament from the chorus. In Shakespeare's plays the messenger's speeches are shorter because violence has already been seen onstage (the description of Ophelia's death in *Hamlet* might be an exception). In all three of his Dublin plays, O'Casey makes use of the ancient Greek convention of a Nuntius who relates solemnly how one of the main characters – Minnie Powell, Johnny Boyle, Jack Clitheroe – met her or his death. In Act Four of *The Plough* Brennan describes the so-called noble end of Jack Clitheroe in language stuffed with conventional platitudes. O'Casey here insists on puncturing the description by having Bessie pour scorn on Brennan's own cowardice, and yet the conventional picture remains to contrast with Nora's demented state. Mrs Gogan has two such formal speeches in Act Four (pp. 89, 98).

It is worth noting here that language is shown up as finally inadequate; the play ends in stalemate. The song that the British soldiers sing merely repeats what the Figure in the Window called for: men to leave hearth and home to fight for their country. The major irony – and all of O'Casey's tragi-comedies end ironically – is that the 'home fires' *are* burning now in Dublin, but burning in destruction and not in domestic security. Because of the Ireland–England divide, the language held in common finally breaks down over the meaning of 'home', the very thing Nora Clitheroe cared most about. Her mad speeches show how dislocated she, as representative Irish woman, now is after the Rising. Her delusion that she is at home waiting for Jack is presented as something non-verbal: Brennan is told to *look* at her, to 'see' the way she is (pp. 83, 85), and how incapable she is of being *told*, of being given the truth in words. The image of Dublin burning thus challenges language and confronts the audience with the tragic irony of 'keeping the home fires burning'.

REFERENCE

Kearney, Colbert, *The Glamour of Grammar: Orality, Politics and the Emergence of Sean O'Casey*, Westport, CT: Greenwood Press, 2000.

Performance

The Plough and the Stars is the most frequently staged of O'Casey's plays and therefore his most successful in performance. It should be remembered that the disturbances at the Abbey in 1926 happened only on the fourth night of the first production; although the play was controversial, it was popular. Productions in London (1926) and New York (1927) were equally well received by the critics, although always, from those premières down to revivals in the 1980s and 1990s, there have been critics who see the play as scrappy, melodramatic and lacking in clarity of theme. Of course, it is the task of the director to bring out the coherence and clarity of the play onstage.

The worst kind of production presents *The Plough* as an aimless entertainment, as if the characters exist in a television situation comedy where there happen to be militaristic noises offstage. But the key to watching or reading *The Plough* lies in the progressively intense rhythm of events. Every play has a rhythm. It may seem merely to 'unroll' in a series of haphazard and varied events, but if it is well written it will organise these events in a design which accumulates like a dynamic jigsaw. It has to be dynamic, because the design cannot be merely pictorial. What happens onstage (which in reading we must try to visualise) is as much like an extended piece of music as it is a picture being completed. As in music, there are slow parts and quick parts, sudden shifts from soft to loud notes, chords which sound themes which will repeat again and again, and a constant beat which holds the whole piece together as it moves towards a climax. In reading *The Plough* we must discover this rhythm. It may help to study the way Act Four brings to a harsh closure many of the themes sounded in Act One. If the reader looks closely at Act Four they will notice that the *mood* is now very different from Act One. In contrast to the lively spirits, the energy of teasing, abuse and delightful sense of life, Act Four is sombre, tense, watchful, the characters constantly having to subdue outbreaks of dispute lest Nora's rest be disrupted, while the presence of the coffin onstage sets the tone for a disturbing sense of death.

A useful way to study this rhythm is to break down an act into micro-units, or what in American theatre are called 'beats'. A beat is a scene within a scene just long enough to contain its own energy. Each beat has its own purpose. For example, in Act Four the first beat is concerned with the card game. While the three men play cards, they discuss what happened to Nora: the game provides a focus for concentration. This is far better than if the three men simply sat around talking. The *ritual* of card-playing paves the way for Nora's ritual of making tea: these normal activities actually increase our sense here of abnormality. The card game, as such, does not matter. Far more important are Mollser's death, Nora's loss of her baby, and Nora's breakdown. By means of the ritualistic card game, then, O'Casey supplies a chorus on the tragic action.

In the next beat Bessie enters to silence the men arguing over the cards. This little scene conveys a sense of urgency and anxiety. We see Bessie in a new light – that of nurse and protector. A third beat follows with the entrance of Brennan, who is looking for Nora. His purpose gives a tension to this little scene: he has a message to deliver. The need of the others to protect Nora from any further bad news means an intensification here of the atmosphere of anxiety generated by the opening of Act Four, with its very important stage directions.

The rhythm is thus building up moment by moment, tightening the screws, so to speak, until the British soldiers enter. Brennan's presence is a threat to the safety of the other three men. The fourth beat, however, comes with Nora's entrance just after Brennan's account of Clitheroe's death and his sentimental assurance that Nora will be proud when she knows 'she has had a hero for a husband' (p. 83). Bessie corrects this view with the declaration that a sight of Nora would disprove any such idea, and it is at just this moment that Nora enters. The purpose, then, is for Nora *visually* to offset Brennan's prediction and in that way to get the audience to sweep away all militaristic propaganda and to invest feeling instead in Nora's victimhood, Nora's representative status as tragic sacrifice.

Some critics have thought the echo of Shakespeare's Ophelia in her mad scene too obvious here, too much of a distraction. But this is not, or ought not to be, so. Madness on stage is a visual matter: it is 'ostension' or showing in iconic form the alienated state of a pathetic figure. When, in this fourth beat, Bessie remarks, 'isn't this pitiful!' (p. 84) the audience's response is being carefully directed. Fluther points out to Brennan what Nora's derangement signifies: 'Now *you can see* th' way she is, man' (p. 85, emphasis added). The Covey repeats this formulation after Bessie leads Nora off again: 'Now *that you've seen* how bad she is . . .' (p. 86). The audience has seen the same thing, and so is actively implicated. A good play will involve the spectators in just this way, the performances on stage combining with this visualisation. They form an ensemble or group concentrating on the deepening mood.

The fifth, brief, beat records Brennan easing himself for protection into the circle of the three card-players. This is followed by the sixth beat when Corporal Stoddart enters. Here the mood shifts abruptly to danger; his purpose is to get the coffin out and do a surveillance of the occupants of the apartment. He is led by the Covey into a discussion of socialism and child mortality versus the perils of warfare.

li

The one detail revealed in this scene is that the Rising is nearly over and was never more than a dog-fight (p. 88). The sound-effects of a sniper's bullet and the eerie cry of 'Ambulance!' immediately throw the Corporal's summary into ironic question. He resolves to find the sniper, and the tension is given another heightening twist. The seventh beat comes with Mrs Gogan's arrival to supervise the removal of the coffin, and here the mood expands to arouse sympathy for her and admiration for Fluther. The beats which follow relate to Bessie's angry assertion of her Protestant identity to Corporal Stoddart, Peter's old irritation over the Covey's teasing, and Fluther's comic acceptance of incarceration in a church so long as the men may play cards.

All of this unrolling action has to be seen as the careful dramatisation of a closing in, a closing down on the people. A constant sense of unease is maintained. In the ninth beat, after the sniper has struck again and Sergeant Tinley has entered in anger, the men are roughly evacuated in a mood of defiance, paving the way for Bessie and Nora's last scene. As before, Bessie is asleep when Nora enters, except that now a street battle is raging offstage and the sense of danger is acute. Bessie's wrestling with Nora results in Bessie being shot directly in front of the window that is upstage-centre, theatrically a commanding position. When the Abbey actress Marie Kean played the next, twelfth, beat in the 1966 television production of *The Plough* she made Bessie's death-scene remarkably moving. This is the only death actually witnessed in the course of a play where many die offstage; therefore, the performance of Bessie's death (as representative and as, again, something *seen*) is crucial to the effect of the ending. Marie Kean prolonged the death-scene (rather as Laurence Olivier prolonged the death of Richard III) so that her every movement, her twisting and crawling, communicated agony and desperation. The audience could not but feel both pity and terror here, as tragedy demands. The death of Bessie marks the absurd and yet the one truly heroic moment in this anti-heroic play, and caused O'Casey much trouble in the writing. Thus its performance is a matter of considerable importance if the effect is to be properly cathartic.

This scene is followed by two more beats, as Mrs Gogan escorts Nora away to her flat and the two British soldiers re-enter. The effect of the final scene is ironic. O'Casey calls for a lighting effect: a '*glare in the sky*' seen through the back window flaring '*into a fuller and a deeper red*' (p. 99). In his notes for the lighting written for the Samuel French acting edition of *The Plough* in 1932, O'Casey explains what is needed: 'Two special red floods on illuminated cloth at window, back; these to be on dimmers, so that red glow rises and falls during Act, to indicate fires in city' (p. 71). The sudden flare into a fuller and deeper red signifies, as Sergeant Tinley says (p. 99), the British attack on the General Post Office, where Pearse, Connolly and the Irish forces are mainly stationed. The game is up. The final song, in which the two soldiers on-stage join, is both an encouragement to this fire of retaliation and a celebration of cheerfulness very much at odds with all that has befallen the tenement dwellers.

The whole of Act Four, then, has relentlessly progressed towards this ironic interrogation of a victory for one side which is also a massive defeat for the other. In performance, the final moments are searingly moving and dismaying. Through that complex ending the audience, and the readers of the text, come to *see* (that word is again crucial) and thus register the folly and the horror of war.

REFERENCE

O'Casey, Sean, *The Plough and the Stars: A Tragedy in Four Acts* [Acting Edition], London: Samuel French, 1932.

THE PLOUGH AND THE STARS

A TRAGEDY IN FOUR ACTS

To the gay laugh of my mother
at the gate of the grave

Characters

Jack Clitheroe (a bricklayer),
  Commandant in the Irish Citizen Army
Nora Clitheroe, his wife
Peter Flynn (a labourer), Nora's uncle
The Young Covey (a fitter), Clitheroe's cousin
Bessie Burgess (a street fruit-vendor)
Mrs Gogan (a charwoman)
Mollser, her consumptive child
Fluther Good (a carpenter)

Residents in the Tenement

Lieut. Langon (a Civil Servant),
  of the Irish Volunteers
Capt. Brennan (a chicken butcher),
  of the Irish Citizen Army
Corporal Stoddart, of the Wiltshires
Sergeant Tinley, of the Wiltshires
Rosie Redmond, a daughter of 'the Digs'
A Bartender
A Woman
The Figure in the Window

Act One – The living-room of the Clitheroe flat in a
  Dublin tenement.
Act Two – A public-house, outside of which a meeting
  is being held.
Act Three – The street outside the Clitheroe tenement.
Act Four – The room of Bessie Burgess.

Time – Acts One and Two, November 1915; Acts Three
  and Four, Easter Week, 1916. A few days elapse
  between Acts Three and Four.

Act One

The home of the Clitheroes. It consists of the front and back drawing-rooms in a fine old Georgian house, struggling for its life against the assaults of time, and the more savage assaults of the tenants. The room shown is the back drawing-room, wide, spacious, and lofty. At back is the entrance to the front drawing-room. The space, originally occupied by folding doors, is now draped with casement cloth of a dark purple, decorated with a design in reddish-purple and cream. One of the curtains is pulled aside, giving a glimpse of front drawing-room, at the end of which can be seen the wide, lofty windows looking out into the street. The room directly in front of the audience is furnished in a way that suggests an attempt towards a finer expression of domestic life. The large fireplace on right is of wood, painted to look like marble (the original has been taken away by the landlord). On the mantelshelf are two candlesticks of dark carved wood. Between them is a small clock. Over the clock is hanging a calendar which displays a picture of The Sleeping Venus. *In the centre of the breast of the chimney hangs a picture of Robert Emmet. On the right of the entrance to the front drawing-room is a copy of* The Gleaners, *on the opposite side a copy of* The Angelus. *Underneath* The Gleaners *is a chest of drawers on which stands a green bowl filled with scarlet dahlias and white chrysanthemums. Near to the fireplace is a settee which at night forms a double bed for Clitheroe and Nora. Underneath* The Angelus *are a number of shelves containing saucepans and a frying-pan. Under these is a table on which are various*

3

*articles of delftware. Near the end of the room, opposite
to the fireplace, is a gate-legged table, covered with a
cloth. On top of the table a huge cavalry sword is lying.
To the right is a door which leads to a lobby from which
the staircase leads to the hall. The floor is covered with
a dark green linoleum. The room is dim except where it
is illuminated from the glow of the fire. Through the
window of the room at back can be seen the flaring of
the flame of a gasolene lamp giving light to workmen
repairing the street. Occasionally can be heard the clang
of crowbars striking the setts. Fluther Good is repairing
the lock of door, right. A claw-hammer is on a chair
beside him, and he has a screwdriver in his hand. He is
a man of forty years of age, rarely surrendering to
thoughts of anxiety, fond of his 'oil' but determined to
conquer the habit before he dies. He is square-jawed and
harshly featured, under the left eye is a scar, and his nose
is bent from a smashing blow received in a fistic battle
long ago. He is bald, save for a few peeping tufts of
reddish hair around his ears; and his upper lip is hidden
by a scrubby red moustache, embroidered here and there
with a grey hair. He is dressed in a seedy black suit,
cotton shirt with a soft collar, and wears a very
respectable little black bow. On his head is a faded jerry
hat, which, when he is excited, he has a habit of
knocking farther back on his head, in a series of taps.
In an argument he usually fills with sound and fury
generally signifying a row. He is in his shirt-sleeves at
present, and wears a soiled white apron, from a pocket
in which sticks a carpenter's two-foot rule. He has just
finished the job of putting on a new lock, and, filled with
satisfaction, he is opening and shutting the door,
enjoying the completion of a work well done. Sitting at
the fire, airing a white shirt, is Peter Flynn. He is a little,
thin bit of a man, with a face shaped like a lozenge; on
his cheeks and under his chin is a straggling wiry beard*

*of a dirty-white and lemon hue. His face invariably
wears a look of animated anguish, mixed with irritated
defiance, as if everybody was at war with him, and he at
war with everybody. He is cocking his head in a way
that suggests resentment at the presence of Fluther, who
pays no attention to him, apparently, but is really
furtively watching him. Peter is clad in a singlet, white
whipcord knee-breeches, and is in his stocking-feet.
A voice is heard speaking outside of door, left (it is that
of Mrs Gogan).*

Mrs Gogan (*outside*) Who are you lookin' for, sir? Who?
Mrs Clitheroe? . . . Oh, excuse me. Oh ay, up this way.
She's out, I think: I seen her goin'. Oh, you've somethin'
for her; oh, excuse me. You're from Arnott's . . . I see . . .
You've a parcel for her . . . Righto . . . I'll take it . . .
give it to her the minute she comes in . . . It'll be quite
safe . . . Oh, sign that . . . Excuse me . . . Where? . . .
Here? . . . No, there; righto. Am I to put Maggie or Mrs?
What is it? You dunno? Oh, excuse me.

*Mrs Gogan opens the door and comes in. She is a
doleful-looking little woman of forty, insinuating
manner and sallow complexion. She is fidgety and
nervous, terribly talkative, has a habit of taking up
things that may be near her and fiddling with them
while she is speaking. Her heart is aflame with
curiosity, and a fly could not come into nor go out of
the house without her knowing. She has a draper's
parcel in her hand, the knot of the twine tying it is
untied. Peter, more resentful of this intrusion than of
Fluther's presence, gets up from the chair, and without
looking around, his head carried at an angry cock,
marches into the room at back.*

(*Removing the paper and opening the cardboard box it
contains*) I wondher what's that now? A hat! (*She takes*

out a hat, black, with decorations in red and gold.) God, she's goin' to th' divil lately for style! That hat, now, cost more than a penny. Such notions of upperosity she's gettin'. (*Putting the hat on her head*) Oh, swank, what! (*She replaces it in parcel.*)

Fluther She's a pretty little Judy, all the same.

Mrs Gogan Ah, she is, an' she isn't. There's prettiness an' prettiness in it. I'm always sayin' that her skirts are a little too short for a married woman. An' to see her, sometimes of an evenin', in her glad-neck gown would make a body's blood run cold. I do be ashamed of me life before her husband. An' th' way she thries to be polite, with her 'Good mornin', Mrs Gogan,' when she's goin' down, an' her 'Good evenin', Mrs Gogan,' when she's comin' up. But there's politeness an' politeness in it.

Fluther They seem to get on well together, all th' same.

Mrs Gogan Ah, they do, an' they don't. The pair o' them used to be like two turtle doves always billin' an' cooin'. You couldn't come into th' room but you'd feel, instinctive like, that they'd just been afther kissin' an' cuddlin' each other . . . It often made me shiver, for, afther all, there's kissin' an' cuddlin' in it. But I'm thinkin' he's beginnin' to take things more quietly; the mysthery of havin' a woman's a mysthery no longer . . . She dhresses herself to keep him with her, but it's no use – afther a month or two, th' wondher of a woman wears off.

Fluther I dunno, I dunno. Not wishin' to say anything derogatory, I think it's all a question of location: when a man finds th' wondher of one woman beginnin' to die, it's usually beginnin' to live in another.

Mrs Gogan She's always grumblin' about havin' to live in a tenement house. 'I wouldn't like to spend me last hour in one, let alone live me life in a tenement,' says she. 'Vaults,' says she, 'that are hidin' th' dead, instead of homes that are sheltherin' th' livin'.' 'Many a good one,' says I , 'was reared in a tenement house.' Oh, you know, she's a well-up little lassie, too; able to make a shillin' go where another would have to spend a pound. She's wipin' th' eyes of th' Covey an' poor oul' Pether – everybody knows that – screwin' every penny she can out o' them, in ordher to turn th' place into a babby-house. An' she has th' life frightened out o' them; washin' their face, combin' their hair, wipin' their feet, brushin' their clothes, thrimmin' their nails, cleanin' their teeth – God Almighty, you'd think th' poor men were undhergoin' penal servitude.

Fluther (*with an exclamation of disgust*) A-a-ah, that's goin' beyond th' beyonds in a tenement house. That's a little bit too derogatory.

> *Peter enters from room, back, head elevated and resentful fire in his eyes; he is still in his singlet and trousers, but is now wearing a pair of unlaced boots – possibly to be decent in the presence of Mrs Gogan. He places the white shirt, which he has carried in on his arm, on the back of a chair near the fire, and, going over to the chest of drawers, he opens drawer after drawer, looking for something; as he fails to find it he closes each drawer with a snap; he pulls out pieces of linen neatly folded, and bundles them back again any way.*

Peter (*in accents of anguish*) Well, God Almighty, give me patience! (*He returns to room, back, giving the shirt a vicious turn as he passes.*)

Mrs Gogan I wondher what he is foostherin' for now?

Fluther He's adornin' himself for th' meeting tonight. (*Pulling a handbill from his pocket and reading*) 'Great

7

Demonstration an' torchlight procession around places in th' city sacred to th' memory of Irish Patriots, to be concluded be a meetin', at which will be taken an oath of fealty to th' Irish Republic. Formation in Parnell Square at eight o'clock.' Well, they can hold it for Fluther. I'm up th' pole; no more dhrink for Fluther. It's three days now since I touched a dhrop, an' I feel a new man already.

Mrs Gogan Isn't oul' Peter a funny-lookin' little man? . . . Like somethin' you'd pick off a Christmas Tree . . . When he's dhressed up in his canonicals, you'd wondher where he'd been got. God forgive me, when I see him in them, I always think he must ha' had a Mormon for a father! He an' th' Covey can't abide each other; th' pair o' them is always at it, thryin' to best each other. There'll be blood dhrawn one o' these days.

Fluther How is it that Clitheroe himself, now, doesn't have anythin' to do with th' Citizen Army? A couple o' months ago, an' you'd hardly ever see him without his gun, an' th' Red Hand o' Liberty Hall in his hat.

Mrs Gogan Just because he wasn't made a Captain of. He wasn't goin' to be in anything where he couldn't be conspishuous. He was so cocksure o' being made one that he bought a Sam Browne belt, an' was always puttin' it on an' standin' in th' door showing it off, till th' man came an' put out th' street lamps on him. God, I think he used to bring it to bed with him! But I'm tellin' you herself was delighted that that cock didn't crow, for she's like a clockin' hen if he leaves her sight for a minute.

While she is talking, she takes up book after book from the table, looks into each of them in a near-sighted way, and then leaves them back. She now lifts up the sword, and proceeds to examine it.

8

Be th' look of it, this must ha' been a general's sword . . .
All th' gold lace an' th' fine figaries on it . . . Sure it's
twiced too big for him.

Fluther A-ah; it's a baby's rattle he ought to have, an' he
as he is with thoughts tossin' in his head of what may
happen to him on th' day o' judgement.

> *Peter has entered, and seeing Mrs Gogan with the*
> *sword, goes over to her, pulls it resentfully out of her*
> *hands, and marches into the room, back, without*
> *speaking.*

Mrs Gogan (*as Peter whips the sword*) Oh, excuse me! . . .
(*To Fluther*) Isn't he th' surly oul' rascal!

Fluther Take no notice of him . . . You'd think he was
dumb, but when you get his goat, or he has a few jars
up, he's vice versa. (*He coughs.*)

Mrs Gogan (*she has now sidled over as far as the shirt*
hanging on the chair) Oh, you've got a cold on you,
Fluther.

Fluther (*carelessly*) Ah, it's only a little one.

Mrs Gogan You'd want to be careful, all th' same.
I knew a woman, a big lump of a woman, red-faced an'
round-bodied, a little awkward on her feet; you'd think,
to look at her, she could put out her two arms an' lift a
two-storeyed house on th' top of her head; got a ticklin'
in her throat, an' a little cough, an' th' next mornin'
she had a little catchin' in her chest, an' they had just
time to wet her lips with a little rum, an' off she went.
(*She begins to look at and handle the shirt.*)

Fluther (*a little nervously*) It's only a little cold I have;
there's nothing derogatory wrong with me.

Mrs Gogan I dunno; there's many a man this minute
lowerin' a pint, thinkin' of a woman, or pickin' out a

winner, or doin' work as you're doin', while th' hearse dhrawn be th' horses with the black plumes is dhrivin' up to his own hall door, an' a voice that he doesn't hear is muttherin' in his ear, 'Earth to earth, an' ashes t' ashes, an' dust to dust.'

Fluther (*faintly*) A man in th' pink o' health should have a holy horror of allowin' thoughts o' death to be festherin' in his mind, for – (*with a frightened cough*) be God, I think I'm afther gettin' a little catch in me chest that time – it's a creepy thing to be thinkin' about.

Mrs Gogan It is, an' it isn't; it's both bad an' good . . . It always gives meself a kind o' thresspassin' joy to feel meself movin' along in a mournin' coach, an me thinkin' that, maybe, th' next funeral'll be me own, an' glad, in a quiet way, that this is somebody else's.

Fluther An' a curious kind of a gaspin' for breath – I hope there's nothin' derogatory wrong with me.

Mrs Gogan (*examining the shirt*) Frills on it, like a woman's petticoat.

Fluther Suddenly gettin' hot, an' then, just as suddenly, gettin' cold.

Mrs Gogan (*holding out the shirt towards Fluther*) How would you like to be wearin' this Lord Mayor's nightdhress, Fluther?

Fluther (*vehemently*) Blast you an' your nightshirt! Is a man fermentin' with fear to stick th' showin' off to him of a thing that looks like a shinin' shroud?

Mrs Gogan Oh, excuse me!

Peter has again entered, and he pulls the shirt from the hands of Mrs Gogan, replacing it on the chair. He returns to room.

Peter (*as he goes out*) Well, God Almighty, give me patience!

Mrs Gogan (*to Peter*) Oh, excuse me!

There is heard a cheer from the men working outside on the street, followed by the clang of tools being thrown down, then silence. The glare of the gasolene light diminishes and finally goes out.

(*Running into the back room to look out of the window*) What's the men repairin' th' streets cheerin' for?

Fluther (*sitting down weakly on a chair*) You can't sneeze but that oul' one wants to know th' why an' th' wherefore . . . I feel as dizzy as bedamned! I hope I didn't give up th' beer too suddenly.

The Covey comes in by door, right. He is about twenty-five, tall, thin, with lines on his face that form a perpetual protest against life as he conceives it to be. Heavy seams fall from each side of nose, down around his lips, as if they were suspenders keeping his mouth from falling. He speaks in a slow, wailing drawl; more rapidly when he is excited. He is dressed in dungarees, and is wearing a vividly red tie. He flings his cap with a gesture of disgust on the table, and begins to take off his overalls.

Mrs Gogan (*to the Covey, as she runs back into the room*) What's after happenin', Covey?

The Covey (*with contempt*) Th' job's stopped. They've been mobilized to march in th' demonstration tonight undher th' Plough an' th' Stars. Didn't you hear them cheerin', th' mugs! They have to renew their political baptismal vows to be faithful *in seculo seculorum*.

Fluther (*forgetting his fear in his indignation*) There's no reason to bring religion into it. I think we ought to have as great a regard for religion as we can, so as to keep it out of as many things as possible.

The Covey (*pausing in the taking off of his dungarees*) Oh, you're one o' the boys that climb into religion as high as a short Mass on Sunday mornin's? I suppose you'll be singin' songs o' Sion an' songs o' Tara at th' meetin', too.

Fluther We're all Irishmen, anyhow; aren't we?

The Covey (*with hand outstretched, and in a professional tone*) Look here, comrade, there's no such thing as an Irishman; or an Englishman, or a German or a Turk; we're all only human bein's. Scientifically speakin', it's all a question of the accidental gatherin' together of mollycewels an' atoms.

Peter comes in with a collar in his hand. He goes over to mirror, left, and proceeds to try to put it on.

Fluther Mollycewels an' atoms! D'ye think I'm goin' to listen to you thryin' to juggle Fluther's mind with complicated cunundhrums of mollycewels an' atoms?

The Covey (*rather loudly*) There's nothin' complicated in it. There's no fear o' th' Church tellin' you that mollycewels is a stickin' together of millions of atoms o' sodium, carbon, potassium o' iodide, etcetera, that, accordin' to th' way they're mixed, make a flower, a fish, a star that you see shinin' in th' sky, or a man with a big brain like me, or a man with a little brain like you!

Fluther (*more loudly still*) There's no necessity to be raisin' your voice; shoutin's no manifestin' forth of a growin' mind.

Peter (*struggling with his collar*) God, give me patience with this thing . . . She makes these collars as stiff with starch as a shinin' band o' solid steel! She does it

purposely to thry an' twart me. If I can't get it on th'
singlet, how, in th' Name o' God, am I goin' to get it on
th' shirt?

The Covey (*loudly*) There's no use o' arguin' with you;
it's education you want, comrade.

Fluther The Covey an' God made th' world, I suppose,
wha'?

The Covey When I hear some men talkin' I'm inclined
to disbelieve that th' world's eight-hundhred million
years old, for it's not long since th' fathers o' some o'
them crawled out o' th' sheltherin' slime o' the sea.

Mrs Gogan (*from room at back*) There, they're afther
formin' fours, an' now they're goin' to march away.

Fluther (*scornfully*) Mollycewels! (*He begins to untie his
apron.*) What about Adam an' Eve?

The Covey Well, what about them?

Fluther (*fiercely*) What about them, you?

The Covey Adam an' Eve! Is that as far as you've got?
Are you still thinkin' there was nobody in th' world
before Adam an' Eve? (*Loudly*) Did you ever hear, man,
of th' skeleton of th' man o' Java?

Peter (*casting the collar from him*) Blast it, blast it, blast
it!

Fluther (*viciously folding his apron*) Ah, you're not goin'
to be let tap your rubbidge o' thoughts into th' mind o'
Fluther.

The Covey You're afraid to listen to th' thruth!

Fluther Who's afraid?

The Covey You are!

Fluther G'way, you wurum!

The Covey Who's a wurum?

Fluther You are, or you wouldn't talk th' way you're talkin'.

The Covey Th' oul', ignorant savage leppin' up in you, when science shows you that th' head of your god is an empty one. Well, I hope you're enjoyin' th' blessin' o' havin' to live be th' sweat of your brow.

Fluther You'll be kickin' an' yellin' for th' priest yet, me boyo. I'm not goin' to stand silent an' simple listenin' to a thick like you makin' a maddenin' mockery o' God Almighty. It 'ud be a nice derogatory thing on me conscience' an' me dyin', to look back in rememberin' shame of talkin' to a word-weavin' little ignorant yahoo of a red flag Socialist!

Mrs Gogan has returned to the front room, and has wandered around looking at things in general, and is now in front of the fireplace looking at the picture hanging over it.

Mrs Gogan For God's sake, Fluther, dhrop it; there's always th' makin's of a row in th' mention of religion . . . (*Looking at picture*) God bless us, it's a naked woman!

Fluther (*coming over to look at it*) What's undher it? (*Reading*) 'Georgina: The Sleepin' Vennis'. Oh, that's a terrible picture; oh, that's a shockin' picture! Oh, th' one that got that taken, she must have been a prime lassie!

Peter (*who also has come over to look, laughing, with his body bent at the waist, and his head slightly tilted back*) Hee, hee, hee, hee, hee!

Fluther (*indignantly, to Peter*) What are you hee, hee-in' for? That's a nice thing to be hee, hee-in' at. Where's your morality, man?

Mrs Gogan God forgive us, it's not right to be lookin' at it.

Fluther It's nearly a derogatory thing to be in th' room where it is.

Mrs Gogan (*giggling hysterically*) I couldn't stop any longer in th' same room with three men, afther lookin' at it!

She goes out. The Covey, who has divested himself of his dungarees, throws them with a contemptuous motion on top of Peter's white shirt.

Peter (*plaintively*) Where are you throwin' them? Are you thryin' to twart an' torment me again?

The Covey Who's thryin' to twart you?

Peter (*flinging the dungarees violently on the floor*) You're not goin' to make me lose me temper, me young Covey.

The Covey (*flinging the white shirt on the floor*) If you're Nora's pet, aself, you're not goin' to get your way in everything.

Peter (*plaintively, with his eyes looking up at the ceiling*) I'll say nothin' . . . I'll leave you to th' day when th' all-pitiful, all-merciful, all-lovin' God 'll be handin' you to th' angels to be rievin' an' roastin' you, tearin' an' tormentin' you, burnin' an' blastin' you!

The Covey Aren't you th' little malignant oul' bastard, you lemon-whiskered oul' swine!

Peter runs to the sword, draws it, and makes for the Covey, who dodges him around the table; Peter has no intention of striking, but the Covey wants to take no chances.

(*Dodging*) Fluther, hold him, there. It's a nice thing to have a lunatic like this lashin' around with a lethal weapon! (*The Covey darts out of the room, right, slamming the door in the face of Peter.*)

Peter (*battering and pulling at the door*) Lemme out, lemme out; isn't it a poor thing for a man who wouldn't say a word against his greatest enemy to have to listen to that Covey's twartin' animosities, shovin' poor, patient people into a lashin' out of curses that darken his soul with th' shadow of th' wrath of th' last day!

Fluther Why d'ye take notice of him? If he seen you didn't, he'd say nothin' derogatory.

Peter I'll make him stop his laughin' an' leerin', jibin' an' jeerin' an' scarifyin' people with his corner-boy insinuations! . . . He's always thryin' to rouse me: if it's not a song, it's a whistle; if it isn't a whistle, it's a cough. But you can taunt an' taunt – I'm laughin' at you; he, hee, hee, hee, hee, heee!

The Covey (*singing through the keyhole*)
    Dear harp o' me counthry, in darkness I found thee,
    The dark chain of silence had hung o'er thee long –

Peter (*frantically*) Jasus, d'ye hear that? D'ye hear him soundin' forth his divil-souled song o' provocation?

The Covey (*singing as before*)
    When proudly, me own island harp, I unbound thee,
    An' gave all thy chords to light, freedom an' song!

Peter (*battering the door*) When I get out I'll do for you, I'll do for you, I'll do for you!

The Covey (*through the keyhole*) Cuckoo-oo!

Nora enters by door, right. She is a young woman of twenty-two, alert, swift, full of nervous energy, and a

little anxious to get on in the world. The firm lines of
her face are considerably opposed by a soft, amorous
mouth and gentle eyes. When her firmness fails her,
she persuades with her feminine charm. She is dressed
in a tailor-made costume, and wears around her neck
a silver fox fur.

Nora (*running in and pushing Peter away from the*
door) Oh, can I not turn me back but th' two o' yous are
at it like a pair o' fightin' cocks! Uncle Peter . . . Uncle
Peter . . . UNCLE PETER!

Peter (*vociferously*) Oh, Uncle Peter, Uncle Peter be
damned! D'ye think I'm goin' to give a free pass to th'
young Covey to turn me whole life into a Holy Manual
o' penances an' martyrdoms?

The Covey (*angrily rushing into the room*) If you won't
exercise some sort o' conthrol over that Uncle Peter o'
yours, there'll be a funeral, an' it won't be me that'll be
in th' hearse!

Nora (*between Peter and the Covey, to the Covey*) Are
yous always goin' to be tearin' down th' little bit of
respectability that a body's thryin' to build up? Am I
always goin' to be havin' to nurse yous into th' hardy
habit o' thryin' to keep up a little bit of appearance?

The Covey Why weren't you here to see th' way he run
at me with th' sword?

Peter What did you call me a lemon-whiskered oul'
swine for?

Nora If th' two o' yous don't thry to make a generous
altheration in your goin's on, an' keep on thryin' t'
inaugurate th' customs o' th' rest o' th' house into this
place, yous can flit into other lodgin's where your
bowsey battlin' 'll meet, maybe, with an encore.

Peter (*to Nora*) Would you like to be called a lemon-whiskered oul' swine?

Nora If you attempt to wag that sword of yours at anybody again, it'll have to be taken off you an' put in a safe place away from babies that don't know th' danger o' them things.

Peter (*at entrance to room, back*) Well, I'm not goin' to let anybody call me a lemon-whiskered oul' swine. (*He goes in.*)

Fluther (*trying the door*) Openin' an' shuttin' now with a well-mannered motion, like a door of a select bar in a high-class pub.

Nora (*to the Covey, as she lays table for tea*) An', once for all, Willie, you'll have to thry to deliver yourself from th' desire of provokin' oul' Pether into a wild forgetfulness of what's proper an' allowable in a respectable home.

The Covey Well, let him mind his own business, then. Yesterday, I caught him hee-hee-in' out of him an' he readin' bits out of Jenersky's *Thesis on th' Origin, Development, an' Consolidation of th' Evolutionary Idea of th' Proletariat.*

Nora Now, let it end at that, for God's sake; Jack'll be in any minute, an' I'm not goin' to have th' quiet of this evenin' tossed about in an everlastin' uproar between you an' Uncle Pether. (To *Fluther*) Well, did you manage to settle th' lock, yet, Mr Good?

Fluther (*opening and shutting door*) It's betther than a new one, now, Mrs Clitheroe; it's almost ready to open and shut of its own accord.

Nora (*giving him a coin*) You're a whole man. How many pints will that get you?

Fluther (*seriously*) Ne'er a one at all, Mrs Clitheroe, for
Fluther's on th' wather waggon now. You could stan'
where you're stannin' chantin', 'Have a glass o' malt,
Fluther; Fluther, have a glass o' malt,' till th' bells would
be ringin' th' ould year out an' th' New Year in, an'
you'd have as much chance o' movin' Fluther as a tune
on a tin whistle would move a deaf man an' he dead.

*As Nora is opening and shutting door, Mrs Bessie
Burgess appears at it. She is a woman of forty,
vigorously built. Her face is a dogged one, hardened
by toil, and a little coarsened by drink. She looks
scornfully and viciously at Nora for a few moments
before she speaks.*

Bessie Puttin' a new lock on her door . . . afraid her
poor neighbours ud break through an' steal . . . (*In a
loud tone*) Maybe, now, they're a damn sight more
honest than your ladyship . . . checkin' th' children
playin' on th' stairs . . . gettin' on th' nerves of your
ladyship . . . Complainin' about Bessie Burgess singin'
her hymns at night, when she has a few up . . . (*She
comes in half-way on the threshold, and screams.*) Bessie
Burgess'll sing whenever she damn well likes!

*Nora tries to shut door, but Bessie violently shoves it
in, and, gripping Nora by the shoulders, shakes her.*

You little over-dressed throllope, you, for one pin I'd
paste th' white face o' you!

Nora (*frightened*) Fluther, Fluther!

Fluther (*running over and breaking the hold of Bessie
from Nora*) Now, now, Bessie, Bessie, leave poor Mrs
Clitheroe alone; she'd do no one any harm, an' minds no
one's business but her own.

Bessie Why is she always thryin' to speak proud things, an' lookin' like a mighty one in th' congregation o' th' people!

Nora sinks frightened on to the couch as Jack Clitheroe enters. He is a tall, well-made fellow of twenty-five. His face has none of the strength of Nora's. It is a face in which is the desire for authority, without the power to attain it.

Clitheroe (*excitedly*) What's up? what's afther happenin'?

Fluther Nothin', Jack. Nothin'. It's all over now. Come on, Bessie, come on.

Clitheroe (*to Nora*) What's wrong, Nora? Did she say anything to you?

Nora She was bargin' out of her, an' I only told her to g'up ower o' that to her own place; an' before I knew where I was, she flew at me like a tiger, an' thried to guzzle me!

Clitheroe (*going to door and speaking to Bessie*) Get up to your own place, Mrs Burgess, and don't you be interferin' with my wife, or it'll be th' worse for you . . . Go on, go on!

Bessie (*as Clitheroe is pushing her out*) Mind who you're pushin', now . . . I attend me place o' worship, anyhow . . . not like some o' them that go to neither church, chapel nor meetin'-house . . . If me son was home from th' threnches he'd see me righted.

Bessie and Fluther depart, and Clitheroe closes the door.

Clitheroe (*going over to Nora, and putting his arm round her*) There, don't mind that old bitch, Nora, darling; I'll soon put a stop to her interferin'.

Nora Some day or another, when I'm here be meself, she'll come in an' do somethin' desperate.

Clitheroe (*kissing her*) Oh, sorra fear of her doin' anythin' desperate. I'll talk to her tomorrow when she's sober. A taste o' me mind that'll shock her into the sensibility of behavin' herself!

Nora gets up and settles the table. She sees the dungarees on the floor and stands looking at them, then she turns to the Covey, who is reading Jenersky's Thesis *at the fire.*

Nora Willie, is that th' place for your dungarees?

The Covey (*getting up and lifting them from the floor*) Ah, they won't do th' floor any harm, will they? (*He carries them into room, back.*)

Nora (*calling*) Uncle Peter, now, Uncle Peter; tea's ready.

Peter and the Covey come in from room, back; they all sit down to tea. Peter is in full dress of the Foresters: green coat, gold braided; white breeches, top boots, frilled shirt. He carries the slouch hat, with the white ostrich plume, and the sword in his hands. They eat for a few moments in silence, the Covey furtively looking at Peter with scorn in his eyes. Peter knows it and is fidgety.

The Covey (*provokingly*) Another cut o' bread, Uncle Peter?

Peter maintains a dignified silence.

Clitheroe It's sure to be a great meetin' tonight. We ought to go, Nora.

Nora (*decisively*) I won't go, Jack; you can go if you wish.

A pause.

The Covey D'ye want th' sugar, Uncle Peter?

Peter (*explosively*) Now, are you goin' to start your thryin' an' your twartin' again?

Nora Now, Uncle Peter, you mustn't be so touchy; Willie has only assed you if you wanted th' sugar.

Peter He doesn't care a damn whether I want th' sugar or no. He's only thryin' to twart me!

Nora (*angrily, to the Covey*) Can't you let him alone, Willie? If he wants the sugar, let him stretch his hand out an' get it himself!

The Covey (*to Peter*) Now, if you want the sugar, you can stretch out your hand and get it yourself!

Clitheroe Tonight is th' first chance that Brennan has got of showing himself off since they made a Captain of him – why, God only knows. It'll be a treat to see him swankin' it at th' head of the Citizen Army carryin' th' flag of the Plough an' th' Stars . . . (*Looking roguishly at Nora*) He was sweet on you, once, Nora?

Nora He may have been . . . I never liked him. I always thought he was a bit of a thick.

The Covey They're bringin' nice disgrace on that banner now.

Clitheroe (*remonstratively*) How are they bringin' disgrace on it?

The Covey (*snappily*) Because it's a Labour flag, an' was never meant for politics . . . What does th' design of th' field plough, bearin' on it th' stars of th' heavenly plough, mean, if it's not Communism? It's a flag that should only be used when we're buildin' th' barricades to fight for a Workers' Republic!

Peter (*with a puff of derision*) P-phuh.

The Covey (*angrily*) What are you phuhin' out o' you for? Your mind is th' mind of a mummy. (*Rising*) I betther go an' get a good place to have a look at Ireland's warriors passin' by. (*He goes into room, left, and returns with his cap.*)

Nora (*to the Covey*) Oh, Willie, brush your clothes before you go.

The Covey Oh, they'll do well enough.

Nora Go an' brush them; th' brush is in th' drawer there.

The Covey goes to the drawer, muttering, gets the brush, and starts to brush his clothes.

The Covey (*singing at Peter, as he does so*)
Oh, where's th' slave so lowly,
Condemn'd to chains unholy,
Who, could he burst his bonds at first,
Would pine beneath them slowly?

We tread th' land that . . . bore us,
Th' green flag glitters . . . o'er us,
Th' friends we've tried are by our side,
An' th' foe we hate . . . before us!

Peter (*leaping to his feet in a whirl of rage*) Now, I'm tellin' you, me young Covey, once for all, that I'll not stick any longer these tittherin' taunts of yours, rovin' around to sing your slights an' slandhers, reddenin' th' mind of a man to th' thinkin' an' sayin' of things that sicken his soul with sin! (*Hysterically; lifting up a cup to fling at the Covey*) Be God, I'll –

Clitheroe (*catching his arm*) Now then, none o' that, none o' that!

23

Nora Uncle Pether, Uncle Pether, UNCLE PETHER!

The Covey (*at the door, about to go out*) Isn't that th' malignant oul' varmint! Lookin' like th' illegitimate son of an illegitimate child of a corporal in th' Mexican army! (*He goes out.*)

Peter (*plaintively*) He's afther leavin' me now in such a state of agitation that I won't be able to do meself justice when I'm marchin' to th' meetin'.

Nora (*jumping up*) Oh, for God's sake, here, buckle your sword on, and go to your meetin', so that we'll have at least one hour of peace! (*She proceeds to belt on the sword.*)

Clitheroe (*irritably*) For God's sake hurry him up ou' o' this, Nora.

Peter Are yous all goin' to thry to start to twart me now?

Nora (*putting on his plumed hat*) S-s-sh. Now, your hat's on, your house is thatched; off you pop! (*She gently pushes him from her.*)

Peter (*going, and turning as he reaches the door*) Now, if that young Covey —

Nora Go on, go on.

> Peter goes. Clitheroe sits down in the lounge, lights a cigarette, and looks thoughtfully into the fire. Nora takes the things from the table, placing them on the chest of drawers. There is a pause, then she swiftly comes over to him and sits beside him.

(*Softly*) A penny for them, Jack!

Clitheroe Me? Oh, I was thinkin' of nothing.

Nora You were thinkin' of th' . . . meetin' . . . Jack. When we were courtin' an' I wanted you to go, you'd say, 'Oh, to hell with meetin's,' an' that you felt lonely in cheerin' crowds when I was absent. An' we weren't a month married when you began that you couldn't keep away from them.

Clitheroe Oh, that's enough about th' meetin'. It looks as if you wanted me to go, th' way you're talkin'. You were always at me to give up th' Citizen Army, an' I gave it up; surely that ought to satisfy you.

Nora Ay, you gave it up – because you got th' sulks when they didn't make a Captain of you. It wasn't for my sake, Jack.

Clitheroe For your sake or no, you're benefitin' by it, aren't you? I didn't forget this was your birthday, did I? (*He puts his arms around her.*) And you liked your new hat; didn't you, didn't you? (*He kisses her rapidly several times.*)

Nora (*panting*) Jack, Jack; please, Jack! I thought you were tired of that sort of thing long ago.

Clitheroe Well, you're finding out now that I amn't tired of it yet, anyhow. Mrs Clitheroe doesn't want to be kissed, sure she doesn't? (*He kisses her again.*) Little, little red-lipped Nora!

Nora (*coquettishly removing his arm from around her*) Oh, yes, your little, little red-lipped Nora's a sweet little girl when th' fit seizes you; but your little, little red-lipped Nora has to clean your boots every mornin', all the same.

Clitheroe (*with a movement of irritation*) Oh, well, if we're goin' to be snotty!

A pause.

Nora It's lookin' like as if it was you that was goin' to be . . . snotty! Bridlin' up with bittherness, th' minute a body attempts t' open her mouth.

Clitheroe Is it any wondher, turnin' a tendher sayin' into a meanin' o' malice an' spite!

Nora It's hard for a body to be always keepin' her mind bent on makin' thoughts that'll be no longer than th' length of your own satisfaction. (*A pause. Standing up*) If we're goin' to dhribble th' time away sittin' here like a pair o' cranky mummies, I'd be as well sewin' or doin' something about th' place.

She looks appealingly at him for a few moments; he doesn't speak. She swiftly sits down beside him, and puts her arm around his neck.

(*Imploringly*) Ah, Jack, don't be so cross!

Clitheroe (*doggedly*) Cross? I'm not cross; I'm not a bit cross. It was yourself started it.

Nora (*coaxingly*) I didn't mean to say anything out o' the way. You take a body up too quickly, Jack. (*In an ordinary tone as if nothing of an angry nature had been said*) You didn't offer me me evenin' allowance yet.

Clitheroe silently takes out a cigarette for her and himself and lights both.

(*Trying to make conversation*) How quiet th' house is now; they must be all out.

Clitheroe (*rather shortly*) I suppose so.

Nora (*rising from the seat*) I'm longin' to show you me new hat, to see what you think of it. Would you like to see it?

Clitheroe Ah, I don't mind.

Nora suppresses a sharp reply, hesitates for a moment, then gets the hat, puts it on, and stands before Clitheroe.

Nora Well, how does Mr Clitheroe like me new hat?

Clitheroe It suits you, Nora, it does right enough.

He stands up, puts his hand beneath her chin, and tilts her head up. She looks at him roguishly. He bends down and kisses her.

Nora Here, sit down, an' don't let me hear another cross word out of you for th' rest o' the night.

They sit down.

Clitheroe (*with his arms around her*) Little, little, red-lipped Nora!

Nora (*with a coaxing movement of her body towards him*) Jack!

Clitheroe (*tightening his arms around her*) Well?

Nora You haven't sung me a song since our honeymoon. Sing me one now, do . . . please, Jack!

Clitheroe What song? 'Since Maggie Went Away'?

Nora Ah, no, Jack, not that; it's too sad. 'When You Said You Loved Me.'

Clearing his throat, Clitheroe thinks for a moment, and then begins to sing. Nora, putting an arm around him, nestles her head on his breast and listens delightedly.

Clitheroe (*singing verses following to the air of 'When You and I Were Young, Maggie'*)
    Th' violets were scenting th' woods, Nora,
        Displaying their charm to th' bee,
    When I first said I lov'd only you, Nora,
        An' you said you lov'd only me!

Th' chestnut blooms gleam'd through th' glade, Nora,
  A robin sang loud from a tree,
When I first said I lov'd only you, Nora,
  An' you said you lov'd only me!

Th' golden-rob'd daffodils shone, Nora,
  An' danc'd in th' breeze on th' lea,
When I first said I lov'd only you, Nora,
  An' you said you lov'd only me!

Th' trees, birds, an' bees sang a song, Nora,
  Of happier transports to be,
When I first said I lov'd only you, Nora,
  An' you said you lov'd only me!

*Nora kisses him. A knock is heard at the door, right;
a pause as they listen. Nora clings closely to Clitheroe.
Another knock, more imperative than the first.*

I wonder who can that be, now?

Nora (*a little nervous*) Take no notice of it, Jack; they'll
go away in a minute.

Another knock, followed by a voice.

Voice Commandant Clitheroe, Commandant Clitheroe,
are you there? A message from General Jim Connolly.

Clitheroe Damn it, it's Captain Brennan.

Nora (*anxiously*) Don't mind him, don't mind, Jack.
Don't break our happiness . . . Pretend we're not in. Let
us forget everything tonight but our two selves!

Clitheroe (*reassuringly*) Don't be alarmed, darling; I'll
just see what he wants, an' send him about his business.

Nora (*tremulously*) No, no. Please, Jack; don't open it.
Please, for your own little Nora's sake!

Clitheroe (*rising to open the door*) Now don't be silly, Nora.

> *Clitheroe opens door, and admits a young man in the full uniform of the Irish Citizen Army – green suit; slouch green hat caught up at one side by a small Red Hand badge; Sam Browne belt, with a revolver in the holster. He carries a letter in his hand. When he comes in he smartly salutes Clitheroe. The young man is Captain Brennan.*

Capt. Brennan (*giving the letter to Clitheroe*) A dispatch from General Connolly.

> *While Clitheroe reads out the letter Brennan's eyes are fixed on Nora, who droops as she sits on the lounge.*

Clitheroe (*reading*) 'Commandant Clitheroe is to take command of the eighth battalion of the ICA which will assemble to proceed to the meeting at nine o'clock. He is to see that all units are provided with full equipment; two days' rations and fifty rounds of ammunition. At two o'clock a.m. the army will leave Liberty Hall for a reconnaissance attack on Dublin Castle. – Com.-Gen. Connolly.' I don't understand this. Why does General Connolly call me Commandant?

Capt. Brennan Th' Staff appointed you Commandant, and th' General agreed with their selection.

Clitheroe When did this happen?

Capt. Brennan A fortnight ago.

Clitheroe How is it word was never sent to me?

Capt. Brennan Word was sent to you . . . I meself brought it.

Clitheroe Who did you give it to, then?

Capt. Brennan (*after a pause*) I think I gave it to Mrs Clitheroe, there.

Clitheroe Nora, d'ye hear that?

Nora makes no answer.

(*There is a note of hardness in his voice.*) Nora . . . Captain Brennan says he brought a letter to me from General Connolly, and that he gave it to you . . . Where is it? What did you do with it?

Nora (*running over to him, and pleadingly putting her arms around him*) Jack, please, Jack, don't go out tonight an' I'll tell you; I'll explain everything . . . Send him away, an' stay with your own little red-lipp'd Nora.

Clitheroe (*removing her arms from around him*) None o' this nonsense, now; I want to know what you did with th' letter.

Nora goes slowly to the lounge and sits down.

(*Angrily*) Why didn't you give me th' letter? What did you do with it? . . . (*He shakes her by the shoulder.*) What did you do with th' letter?

Nora (*flaming up*) I burned it, I burned it! That's what I did with it! Is General Connolly an' th' Citizen Army goin' to be your only care? Is your home goin' to be only a place to rest in? Am I goin' to be only somethin' to provide merry-makin' at night for you? Your vanity'll be th' ruin of you an' me yet . . . That's what's movin' you: because they've made an officer of you, you'll make a glorious cause of what you're doin', while your little red-lipp'd Nora can go on sittin' here, makin' a companion of th' loneliness of th' night!

Clitheroe (*fiercely*) You burned it, did you? (*He grips her arm.*) Well, me good lady –

Nora Let go – you're hurtin' me!

Clitheroe You deserve to be hurt . . . Any letter that comes to me for th' future, take care that I get it . . . D'ye hear – take care that I get it!

He goes to the chest of drawers and takes out a Sam Browne belt, which he puts on, and then puts a revolver in the holster. He puts on his hat, and looks towards Nora. While this dialogue is proceeding, and while Clitheroe prepares himself, Brennan softly whistles 'The Soldiers' Song'.

(*At door, about to go out*) You needn't wait up for me; if I'm in at all, it won't be before six in th' morning.

Nora (*bitterly*) I don't care if you never come back!

Clitheroe (*to Capt. Brennan*) Come along, Ned.

They go out. There is a pause. Nora pulls the new hat from her head and with a bitter movement flings it to the other end of the room. There is a gentle knock at door, right, which opens, and Mollser comes into the room. She is about fifteen, but looks to be only about ten, for the ravages of consumption have shrivelled her up. She is pitifully worn, walks feebly, and frequently coughs. She goes over to Nora.

Mollser (*to Nora*) Mother's gone to th' meetin', an' I was feelin' terrible lonely, so I come down to see if you'd let me sit with you, thinkin' you mightn't be goin' yourself . . . I do be terrible afraid I'll die sometime when I'm be meself . . . I often envy you, Mrs Clitheroe, seein' th' health you have, an' th' lovely place you have here, an' wondherin' if I'll ever be sthrong enough to be keepin' a home together for a man. Oh, this must be some more o' the Dublin Fusiliers flyin' off to the front.

*Just before Mollser ceases to speak, there is heard in
the distance the music of a brass band playing a
regiment to the boat on the way to the front. The tune
that is being played is 'It's a Long Way to Tipperary';
as the band comes to the chorus, the regiment is
swinging into the street by Nora's house, and the
voices of the soldiers can be heard lustily singing the
chorus of the song.*

Soldiers (*off*)
It's a long way to Tipperary, it's a long way to go;
It's a long way to Tipperary, to th' sweetest girl I know!
Goodbye Piccadilly, farewell Leicester Square.
It's a long, long way to Tipperary, but my heart's
    right there!

*Nora and Mollser remain silently listening. As the
chorus ends and the music is faint in the distance
again, Bessie Burgess appears at door, right, which
Mollser has left open.*

Bessie (*speaking in towards the room*) There's th' men
marchin' out into th' dhread dimness o' danger, while th'
lice is crawlin' about feedin' on th' fatness o' the land!
But yous'll not escape from th' arrow that flieth be night,
or th' sickness that wasteth be day . . . An' ladyship an'
all, as some o' them may be, they'll be scattered abroad,
like th' dust in th' darkness!

*Bessie goes away; Nora steals over and quietly shuts
the door. She comes back to the lounge and wearily
throws herself on it beside Mollser.*

Mollser (*after a pause and a cough*) Is there anybody
goin', Mrs Clitheroe, with a titther o' sense?

Curtain.

Act Two

*A commodious public-house at the corner of the street in
which the meeting is being addressed from Platform No. 1.
It is the south corner of the public-house that is visible
to the audience. The counter, beginning at back about
one-fourth of the width of the space shown, comes
across two-thirds of the length of the stage, and, taking
a circular sweep, passes out of sight to left. On the
counter are beer-pulls, glasses, and a carafe. The other
three-fourths of the back is occupied by a tall, wide,
two-paned window. Beside this window at the right is
a small, boxlike, panelled snug. Next to the snug is a
double swing door, the entrance to that particular end
of the house. Farther on is a shelf on which customers
may rest their drinks. Underneath the windows is a
cushioned seat. Behind the counter at back can be seen
the shelves running the whole length of the counter.
On these shelves can be seen the end (or the beginning)
of rows of bottles. The Barman is seen wiping the part
of the counter which is in view. Rosie is standing at the
counter toying with what remains of a half of whiskey in
a wineglass. She is a sturdy, well-shaped girl of twenty;
pretty, and pert in manner. She is wearing a cream
blouse, with an obviously suggestive glad neck; a grey
tweed dress, brown stockings and shoes. The blouse and
most of the dress are hidden by a black shawl. She has
no hat, and in her hair is jauntily set a cheap, glittering,
jewelled ornament. It is an hour later.*

Barman (*wiping counter*) Nothin' much doin' in your
line tonight, Rosie?

Rosie Curse o' God on th' haporth, hardly, Tom. There isn't much notice taken of a pretty petticoat of a night like this . . . They're all in a holy mood. Th' solemn-lookin' dials on th' whole o' them an' they marchin' to th' meetin'. You'd think they were th' glorious company of th' saints, an' th' noble army of martyrs thrampin' through th' sthreets of paradise. They're all thinkin' of higher things than a girl's garthers . . . It's a tremendous meetin'; four platforms they have – there's one o' them just outside opposite th' window.

Barman Oh, ay; sure when th' speaker comes (*motioning with his hand*) to th' near end, here, you can see him plain, an' hear nearly everythin' he's spoutin' out of him.

Rosie It's no joke thryin' to make up fifty-five shillin's a week for your keep an' laundhry, an' then taxin' you a quid for your own room if you bring home a friend for th' night . . . If I could only put by a couple of quid for a swankier outfit, everythin' in th' garden ud look lovely –

Barman Whisht, till we hear what he's sayin'.

Through the window is silhouetted the figure of a tall man who is speaking to the crowd. The Barman and Rosie look out of the window and listen.

Voice of the Man It is a glorious thing to see arms in the hands of Irishmen. We must accustom ourselves to the thought of arms, we must accustom ourselves to the sight of arms, we must accustom ourselves to the use of arms . . . Bloodshed is a cleansing and sanctifying thing, and the nation that regards it as the final horror has lost its manhood . . . There are many things more horrible than bloodshed, and slavery is one of them!

The figure moves away towards the right, and is lost to sight and hearing.

Rosie It's th' sacred thruth, mind you, what that man's afther sayin'.

Barman If I was only a little younger, I'd be plungin' mad into th' middle of it!

Rosie (*who is still looking out of the window*) Oh, here's the two gems runnin' over again for their oil!

Peter and Fluther enter tumultuously. They are hot, and full and hasty with the things they have seen and heard. Emotion is bubbling up in them, so that when they drink, and when they speak, they drink and speak with the fullness of emotional passion. Peter leads the way to the counter.

Peter (*splutteringly to the Barman*) Two halves . . . (*To Fluther*) A meetin' like this always makes me feel as if I could dhrink Loch Erinn dhry!

Fluther You couldn't feel any way else at a time like this when th' spirit of a man is pulsin' to be out fightin' for th' thruth with his feet thremblin' on th' way, maybe to th' gallows, an' his ears tinglin' with th' faint, far-away sound of burstin' rifle-shots that'll maybe whip th' last little shock o' life out of him that's left lingerin' in his body!

Peter I felt a burnin' lump in me throat when I heard th' band playin' 'The Soldiers' Song', rememberin' last hearin' it marchin' in military formation, with th' people starin' on both sides at us, carryin' with us th' pride an' resolution o' Dublin to th' grave of Wolfe Tone.

Fluther Get th' Dublin men goin' an' they'll go on full force for anything that's thryin' to bar them away from what they're wantin', where th' slim thinkin' counthry boyo ud limp away from th' first faintest touch of compromisation!

35

Peter (*hurriedly to the Barman*) Two more, Tom! . . .
(*To Fluther*) Th' memory of all th' things that was done,
an' all th' things that was suffered be th' people, was
boomin' in me brain . . . Every nerve in me body was
quiverin' to do somethin' desperate!

Fluther Jammed as I was in th' crowd, I listened to th'
speeches pattherin' on th' people's head, like rain fallin'
on th' corn; every derogatory thought went out o' me
mind, an' I said to meself, 'You can die now, Fluther, for
you've seen th' shadow-dhreams of th' past leppin' to life
in th' bodies of livin' men that show, if we were without
a titther o' courage for centuries, we're vice versa now!'
Looka here. (*He stretches out his arm under Peter's face
and rolls up his sleeve.*) The blood was BOILIN' in me
veins!

*The silhouette of the tall figure again moves into the
frame of the window speaking to the people.*

Peter (*unaware, in his enthusiasm, of the speaker's
appearance, to Fluther*) I was burnin' to dhraw me
sword, an' wave an' wave it over me –

Fluther (*overwhelming Peter*) Will you stop your
blatherin' for a minute, man, an' let us hear what he's
sayin'!

Voice of the Man Comrade soldiers of the Irish Volunteers
and of the Citizen Army, we rejoice in this terrible war.
The old heart of the earth needed to be warmed with the
red wine of the battlefields . . . Such august homage was
never offered to God as this: the homage of millions of
lives given gladly for love of country. And we must be
ready to pour out the same red wine in the same glorious
sacrifice, for without shedding of blood there is no
redemption!

The figure moves out of sight and hearing.

Fluther (*gulping down the drink that remains in his glass, and rushing out*) Come on, man; this is too good to be missed!

Peter finishes his drink less rapidly, and as he is going out wiping his mouth with the back of his hand he runs into the Covey coming in. He immediately erects his body like a young cock, and with his chin thrust forward, and a look of venomous dignity on his face, he marches out.

The Covey (*at counter*) Give us a glass o' malt, for God's sake, till I stimulate meself from th' shock o' seein' th' sight that's afther goin' out!

Rosie (*all business, coming over to the counter, and standing near the Covey*) Another one for me, Tommy; (*to the Barman*) th' young gentleman's ordherin' it in th' corner of his eye.

The Barman brings the drink for the Covey, and leaves it on the counter. Rosie whips it up.

Barman Ay, houl' on there, houl' on there, Rosie!

Rosie (*to the Barman*) What are you houldin' on out o' you for? Didn't you hear th' young gentleman say that he couldn't refuse anything to a nice little bird? (*To the Covey*) Isn't that right, Jiggs? (*The Covey says nothing.*) Didn't I know, Tommy, it would be all right? It takes Rosie to size a young man up, an' tell th' thoughts that are thremblin' in his mind. Isn't that right, Jiggs?

The Covey stirs uneasily, moves a little farther away, and pulls his cap over his eyes.

(*Moving after him*) Great meetin' that's gettin' held outside. Well, it's up to us all, anyway, to fight for our freedom.

The Covey (*to Barman*) Two more, please. (*To Rosie*) Freedom! What's th' use o' freedom, if it's not economic freedom?

Rosie (*emphasizing with extended arm and moving finger*) I used them very words just before you come in. 'A lot o' thricksters,' says I, 'that wouldn't know what freedom was if they got it from their mother.' . . . (*To Barman*) Didn't I, Tommy?

Barman I disremember.

Rosie No, you don't disremember. Remember you said, yourself, it was all 'only a flash in th' pan'. Well, 'flash in th' pan, or no flash in th' pan,' says I, 'they're not goin' to get Rosie Redmond,' says I, 'to fight for freedom that wouldn't be worth winnin' in a raffle!'

The Covey There's only one freedom for th' workin' man: conthrol o' th' means o' production, rates of exchange, an' th' means of disthribution. (*Tapping Rosie on the shoulder*) Look here, comrade, I'll leave here tomorrow night for you a copy of Jenersky's *Thesis on the Origin, Development, an' Consolidation of the Evolutionary Idea of the Proletariat.*

Rosie (*throwing off her shawl on to the counter, and showing an exemplified glad neck, which reveals a good deal of a white bosom*) If y'ass Rosie, it's heartbreakin' to see a young fella thinkin' of anything, or admirin' anything, but silk transparent stockin's showin' off the shape of a little lassie's legs!

The Covey, frightened, moves a little away.

(*Following on*) Out in th' park in th' shade of a warm summery evenin', with your little darlin' bridie to be, kissin' an' cuddlin' (*she tries to put her arm around his neck*), kissin' an' cuddlin', ay?

The Covey (*frightened*) Ay, what are you doin'? None o' that, now; none o' that. I've something else to do besides shinannickin' afther Judies!

He turns away, but Rosie follows, keeping face to face with him.

Rosie Oh, little duckey, oh, shy little duckey! Never held a mot's hand, an' wouldn't know how to tittle a little Judy! (*She clips him under the chin.*) Tittle him undher th' chin, tittle him undher th' chin!

The Covey (*breaking away and running out*) Ay, go on, now; I don't want to have any meddlin' with a lassie like you!

Rosie (*enraged*) Jasus, it's in a monasthery some of us ought to be, spendin' our holidays kneelin' on our adorers, tellin' our beads, an' knockin' hell out of our buzzums!

The Covey (*outside*) Cuckoo-oo!

Peter and Fluther come in again, followed by Mrs Gogan, carrying a baby in her arms. They go over to the counter.

Peter (*with plaintive anger*) It's terrible that young Covey can't let me pass without proddin' at me! Did you hear him murmurin' 'cuckoo' when we were passin'?

Fluther (*irritably*) I wouldn't be everlastin' cockin' me ear to every little whisper that was floatin' around about me! It's my rule never to lose me temper till it would be dethrimental to keep it. There's nothin' derogatory in th' use o' th' word 'cuckoo', is there?

Peter (*tearfully*) It's not th' word; it's th' way he says it: he never says it straight out, but murmurs it with curious quiverin' ripples, like variations on a flute!

Fluther Ah, what odds if he gave it with variations on a thrombone! (*To Mrs Gogan*) What's yours goin' to be, ma'am?

Mrs Gogan Ah, a half o' malt, Fluther.

Fluther (*to Barman*) Three halves, Tommy.

The Barman brings the drinks.

Mrs Gogan (*drinking*) The Foresthers' is a gorgeous dhress! I don't think I've seen nicer, mind you, in a pantomime . . . Th' loveliest part of th' dhress, I think, is th' osthrichess plume . . . When yous are goin' along, an' I see them wavin' an' noddin' an' waggin', I seem to be lookin' at each of yous hangin' at th' end of a rope, your eyes bulgin' an' your legs twistin' an' jerkin', gaspin' an' gaspin' for breath while yous are thryin' to die for Ireland!

Fluther If any o' them is hangin' at the end of a rope, it won't be for Ireland!

Peter Are you goin' to start th' young Covey's game o' proddin' an' twartin' a man? There's not many that's talkin' can say that for twenty-five years he never missed a pilgrimage to Bodenstown!

Fluther You're always blowin' about goin' to Bodenstown. D'ye think no one but yourself ever went to Bodenstown?

Peter (*plaintively*) I'm not blowin' about it; but there's not a year that I go there but I pluck a leaf off Tone's grave, an' this very day me prayer-book is nearly full of them.

Fluther (*scornfully*) Then Fluther has a vice versa opinion of them that put ivy leaves into their prayer-books, scabbin' it on th' clergy, an' thryin' to out-do th' haloes o' th' saints be lookin' as if he was wearin' around his head a glittherin' aroree boree allis! (*Fiercely*) Sure, I don't care a damn if you slep' in Bodenstown! You can take your breakfast, dinner, an' tea on th' grave in Bodenstown, if you like, for Fluther!

Mrs Gogan Oh, don't start a fight, boys, for God's sake; I was only sayin' what a nice costume it is – nicer than th' kilts, for, God forgive me, I always think th' kilts is hardly decent.

Fluther Ah, sure, when you'd look at him, you'd wondher whether th' man was makin' fun o' th' costume, or th' costume was makin' fun o' th' man!

Barman Now, then, thry to speak asy, will yous? We don't want no shoutin' here.

The Covey, followed by Bessie Burgess, comes in. They go over to the opposite end of the counter, and direct their gaze on the other group.

The Covey (*to Barman*) Two glasses o' malt.

Peter There he is, now; I knew he wouldn't be long till he folleyed me in.

Bessie (*speaking to the Covey, but really at the other party*) I can't for th' life o' me undherstand how they can call themselves Catholics, when they won't lift a finger to help poor little Catholic Belgium.

Mrs Gogan (*raising her voice*) What about poor little Catholic Ireland?

Bessie (*over to Mrs Gogan*) You mind your own business, ma'am, an' stupefy your foolishness be gettin' dhrunk.

Peter (*anxiously*) Take no notice of her; pay no attention to her. She's just tormentin' herself towards havin' a row with somebody.

41

Bessie There's a storm of anger tossin' in me heart, thinkin' of all th' poor Tommies, an' with them me own son, dhrenched in water an' soaked in blood, gropin' their way to a shattherin' death, in a shower o' shells! Young men with th' sunny lust o' life beamin' in them, layin' down their white bodies, shredded into torn an' bloody pieces, on th' althar that God Himself has built for th' sacrifice of heroes!

Mrs Gogan Isn't it a nice thing to have to be listenin' to a lassie an' hangin' our heads in a dead silence, knowin' that some persons think more of a ball of malt than they do of th' blessed saints.

Fluther Whisht; she's always dangerous an' derogatory when she's well oiled. Th' safest way to hindher her from havin' any enjoyment out of her spite, is to dip our thoughts into the fact of her bein' a female person that has moved out of th' sight of ordinary sensible people.

Bessie To look at some o' th' women that's knockin' about, now, is a thing to make a body sigh . . . A woman on her own, dhrinkin' with a bevy o' men, is hardly an example to her sex . . . A woman dhrinkin' with a woman is one thing, an' a woman dhrinkin' with herself is still a woman – flappers may be put in another category altogether – but a middle-aged married woman makin' herself th' centre of a circle of men is as a woman that is loud an' stubborn, whose feet abideth not in her own house.

The Covey (*to Bessie*) When I think of all th' problems in front o' th' workers, it makes me sick to be lookin' at oul' codgers goin' about dhressed up like green-accoutred figures gone asthray out of a toyshop!

Peter Gracious God, give me patience to be listenin' to that blasted young Covey proddin' at me from over at th' other end of th' shop!

Mrs Gogan (*dipping her finger in the whiskey, and moistening with it the lips of her baby*) Cissie Gogan's a woman livin' for nigh on twenty-five years in her own room, an' beyond biddin' th' time o' day to her neighbours, never yet as much as nodded her head in th' direction of other people's business, while she knows some as are never content unless they're standin' senthry over other people's doin's!

Bessie is about to reply, when the tall, dark figure is again silhouetted against the window, and the voice of the Speaker is heard speaking passionately.

Voice of Speaker The last sixteen months have been the most glorious in the history of Europe. Heroism has come back to the earth. War is a terrible thing, but war is not an evil thing. People in Ireland dread war because they do not know it. Ireland has not known the exhilaration of war for over a hundred years. When war comes to Ireland she must welcome it as she would welcome the Angel of God! (*The figure passes out of sight and hearing.*)

The Covey (*towards all present*) Dope, dope. There's only one war worth havin': th' war for th' economic emancipation of th' proletariat.

Bessie They may crow away out o' them; but it ud be fitther for some o' them to mend their ways, an' cease from havin' scouts out watchin' for th' comin' of th' Saint Vincent de Paul man, for fear they'd be nailed lowerin' a pint of beer, mockin' th' man with an angel face, shinin' with th' glamour of deceit an' lies!

Mrs Gogan An' a certain lassie standin' stiff behind her own door with her ears cocked listenin' to what's being said, stuffed till she's sthrained with envy of a neighbour thryin' for a few little things that may be got be hard sthrivin' to keep up to th' letther an' th' law, an' th' practices of th' Church!

Peter (*to Mrs Gogan*) If I was you, Mrs Gogan, I'd parry her jabbin' remarks be a powerful silence that'll keep her tantalizin' words from penethratin' into your feelin's. It's always betther to leave these people to th' vengeance o' God!

Bessie Bessie Burgess doesn't put up to know much, never havin' a swaggerin' mind, thanks be to God, but goin' on packin' up knowledge accordin' to her conscience: precept upon precept, line upon line; here a little, an' there a little. But (*with a passionate swing of her shawl*), thanks be to Christ, she knows when she was got, where she was got, an' how she was got; while there's some she knows, decoratin' their finger with a well-polished weddin' ring, would be hard put to it if they were assed to show their weddin' lines!

Mrs Gogan (*plunging out into the centre of the floor in a wild tempest of hysterical rage*) Y' oul' rip of a blasted liar, me weddin' ring's been well earned be twenty years be th' side o' me husband, now takin' his rest in heaven, married to me be Father Dempsey, in th' Chapel o' Saint Jude's, in th' Christmas Week of eighteen hundhred an' ninety-five; an' any kid, livin' or dead, that Jinnie Gogan's had since, was got between th' bordhers of th' Ten Commandments! . . . An' that's more than some o' you can say that are kep' from th' dhread o' desthruction be a few drowsy virtues, that th' first whisper of temptation lulls into a sleep, that'll know one sin from another only on th' day of their last anointin', an' that use th' innocent light o' th' shinin' stars to dip into th' sins of a night's diversion!

Bessie (*jumping out to face Mrs Gogan, and bringing the palms of her hands together in sharp claps to emphasize her remarks*) Liar to you, too, ma'am, y' oul' hardened thresspasser on other people's good nature, wizenin' up your soul in th' arts o' dodgeries, till every dhrop of respectability in a female is dhried up in her, lookin' at your ready-made manoeuverin' with th' menkind!

Barman Here, there; here, there; speak asy there. No rowin' here, no rowin' here, now.

Fluther (*trying to calm Mrs Gogan*) Now Jinnie, Jinnie, it's a derogatory thing to be smirchin' a night like this with a row; it's rompin' with th' feelin's of hope we ought to be, instead o' bein' vice versa!

Peter (*trying to quiet Bessie*) I'm terrible dawny, Mrs Burgess, an' a fight leaves me weak for a long time afterwards . . . Please, Mrs Burgess, before there's damage done, thry to have a little respect for yourself.

Bessie (*with a push of her hand that sends Peter tottering to the end of the shop*) G'way, you little sermonizing, little yella-faced, little consequential, little pudgy, little bum, you!

Mrs Gogan (*screaming*) Fluther, leggo! I'm not goin' to keep an unresistin' silence, an' her scattherin' her festherin' words in me face, stirrin' up every dhrop of decency in a respectable female, with her restless rally o' lies that would make a saint say his prayer backwards!

Bessie (*shouting*) Ah, everybody knows well that th' best charity that can be shown to you is to hide th' thruth as much as our thrue worship of God Almighty will allow us!

Mrs Gogan (*frantically*) Here, houl' th' kid, one o' yous; houl' th' kid for a minute! There's nothin' for it but to show this lassie a lesson or two . . . (*To Peter*) Here, houl' th' kid, you. (*Before Peter is aware of it, she places the infant in his arms. To Bessie, standing before her in a fighting attitude*) Come on, now, me loyal lassie, dyin'

with grief for little Catholic Belgium! When Jinnie
Gogan's done with you, you'll have a little leisure lyin'
down to think an' pray for your king an' counthry!

Barman (*coming from behind the counter, getting
between the women, and proceeding to push them
towards the door*) Here, now, since yous can't have a
little friendly argument quietly, you'll get out o' this
place in quick time. Go on, an' settle your differences
somewhere else – I don't want to have another
endorsement on me licence.

Peter (*anxiously, over to Mrs Gogan*) Here, take your
kid back, ower this. How nicely I was picked, now, for
it to be plumped into me arms!

The Covey She knew who she was givin' it to, maybe.

Peter (*hotly to the Covey*) Now, I'm givin' you fair
warnin', me young Covey, to quit firin' your jibes an'
jeers at me . . . For one o' these days, I'll run out in front
o' God Almighty an' take your sacred life!

Barman (*pushing Bessie out after Mrs Gogan*) Go on,
now; out you go.

Bessie (*as she goes out*) If you think, me lassie, that Bessie
Burgess has an untidy conscience, she'll soon show you
to th' differ!

Peter (*leaving the baby down on the floor*) Ay, be Jasus,
wait there, till I give her back her youngster! (*He runs to
the door.*) Ay, there, ay! (*He comes back.*) There, she's
afther goin' without her kid. What are we goin' to do
with it, now?

The Covey What are we goin' to do with it? Bring it
outside an' show everybody what you're afther findin'!

Peter (*in a panic to Fluther*) Pick it up, you, Fluther, an'
run afther her with it, will you?

46

Fluther What d'ye take Fluther for? You must think Fluther's a right gom. D'ye think Fluther's like yourself, destitute of a titther of undherstandin'?

Barman (*imperatively to Peter*) Take it up, man, an' run out afther her with it, before she's gone too far. You're not goin' to leave th' bloody thing here, are you?

Peter (*plaintively, as he lifts up the baby*) Well, God Almighty, give me patience with all th' scorners, tormentors, an' twarters that are always an' ever thryin' to goad me into prayin' for their blindin' an' blastin' an' burnin' in th' world to come! (*He goes out.*)

Fluther God, it's a relief to get rid o' that crowd. Women is terrible when they start to fight. There's no holdin' them back. (*To the Covey*) Are you goin' to have anything?

The Covey Ah, I don't mind if I have another half.

Fluther (*to Barman*) Two more, Tommy, me son.

The Barman gets the drinks.

You know, there's no conthrollin' a woman when she loses her head.

Rosie enters and goes over to the counter on the side nearest to Fluther.

Rosie (*to Barman*) Divil a use o' havin' a thrim little leg on a night like this; things was never worse . . . Give us a half till tomorrow, Tom, duckey.

Barman (*coldly*) No more tonight, Rosie; you owe me for three already.

Rosie (*combatively*) You'll be paid, won't you?

Barman I hope so.

Rosie You hope so! Is that th' way with you, now?

Fluther (*to Barman*) Give her one; it'll be all right.

Rosie (*clapping Fluther on the back*) Oul' sport!

Fluther Th' meetin' should be soon over, now.

The Covey Th' sooner th' betther. It's all a lot o' blasted nonsense, comrade.

Fluther Oh, I wouldn't say it was all nonsense. Afther all, Fluther can remember th' time, an' him only a dawny chiselur, bein' taught at his mother's knee to be faithful to th' Shan Van Vok!

The Covey That's all dope, comrade; th' sort o' thing that workers are fed on be th' Boorzwawzee.

Fluther (*a little sharply*) What's all dope? Though I'm sayin' it that shouldn't: (*catching his cheek with his hand, and pulling down the flesh from the eye*) d'ye see that mark there, undher me eye? . . . A sabre slice from a dragoon in O'Connell Street! (*Thrusting his head forward towards Rosie*) Feel that dint in th' middle o' me nut!

Rosie (*rubbing Fluther's head, and winking at the Covey*) My God, there's a holla!

Fluther (*putting on his hat with quiet pride*) A skelp from a bobby's baton at a Labour meetin' in th' Phoenix Park!

The Covey He must ha' hitten you in mistake. I don't know what you ever done for th' Labour Movement.

Fluther (*loudly*) D'ye not? Maybe, then, I done as much, an' know as much about th' Labour Movement as th' chancers that are blowin' about it!

Barman Speak easy, Fluther, thry to speak easy.

The Covey There's no necessity to get excited about it, comrade.

Fluther (*more loudly*) Excited? Who's gettin' excited? There's no one gettin' excited! It would take something more than a thing like you to flutther a feather o' Fluther. Blatherin', an', when all is said, you know as much as th' rest in th' wind up!

The Covey Well, let us put it to th' test, then, an' see what you know about th' Labour Movement: what's the mechanism of exchange?

Fluther (*roaring, because he feels he is beaten*) How th' hell do I know what it is? There's nothin' about that in th' rules of our Thrades Union!

Barman For God's sake, thry to speak easy, Fluther.

The Covey What does Karl Marx say about th' Relation of Value to th' Cost o' Production?

Fluther (*angrily*) What th' hell do I care what he says? I'm Irishman enough not to lose me head be follyin' foreigners!

Barman Speak easy, Fluther.

The Covey It's only waste o' time talkin' to you, comrade.

Fluther Don't be comradin' me, mate. I'd be on me last legs if I wanted you for a comrade.

Rosie (*to the Covey*) It seems a highly rediculous thing to hear a thing that's only an inch or two away from a kid, swingin' heavy words about he doesn't know th' meanin' of, an' uppishly thryin' to down a man like Misther Fluther here, that's well flavoured in th' knowledge of th' world he's livin' in.

The Covey (*savagely to Rosie*) Nobody's askin' you to be buttin' in with your prate . . . I have you well taped, me lassie . . . Just you keep your opinions for your own place . . . It'll be a long time before th' Covey takes any insthructions or reprimandin' from a prostitute!

Rosie (*wild with humiliation*) You louse, you louse, you! . . . You're no man . . . You're no man . . . I'm a woman, anyhow, an' if I'm a prostitute aself, I have me feelin's . . . Thryin' to put his arm around me a minute ago, an' givin' me th' glad eye, th' little wrigglin' lump o' desolation turns on me now, because he saw there was nothin' doin' . . . You louse, you! If I was a man, or you were a woman, I'd bate th' puss o' you!

Barman Ay, Rosie, ay! You'll have to shut your mouth altogether, if you can't learn to speak easy!

Fluther (*to Rosie*) Houl' on there, Rosie; houl' on there. There's no necessity to flutther yourself when you're with Fluther . . . Any lady that's in th' company of Fluther is goin' to get a fair hunt . . . This is outside your province . . . I'm not goin' to let you demean yourself be talkin' to a tittherin' chancer . . . Leave this to Fluther – this is a man's job. (*To the Covey*) Now, if you've anything to say, say it to Fluther, an', let me tell you, you're not goin' to be pass-remarkable to any lady in my company.

The Covey Sure I don't care if you were runnin' all night afther your Mary o' th' Curlin' Hair, but, when you start tellin' luscious lies about what you done for th' Labour Movement, it's nearly time to show y'up!

Fluther (*fiercely*) Is it you show Fluther up? G'way, man, I'd beat two o' you before me breakfast!

The Covey (*contemptuously*) Tell us where you bury your dead, will you?

Fluther (*with his face stuck into the face of the Covey*) Sing a little less on th' high note, or, when I'm done with

you, you'll put a Christianable consthruction on things,
I'm tellin' you!

The Covey You're a big fella, you are.

Fluther (*tapping the Covey threateningly on the shoulder*)
Now, you're temptin' Providence when you're temptin'
Fluther!

The Covey (*losing his temper, and bawling*) Easy with
them hands, there, easy with them hands! You're startin'
to take a little risk when you commence to paw the
Covey!

> *Fluther suddenly springs into the middle of the shop,
> flings his hat into the corner, whips off his coat, and
> begins to paw the air.*

Fluther (*roaring at the top of his voice*) Come on, come
on, you lowser; put your mits up now, if there's a man's
blood in you! Be God, in a few minutes you'll see some
snots flyin' around, I'm tellin' you . . . When Fluther's
done with you, you'll have a vice versa opinion of him!
Come on, now, come on!

Barman (*running from behind the counter and catching
hold of the Covey*) Here, out you go, me little bowsey.
Because you got a couple o' halves you think you can act
as you like. (*He pushes the Covey to the door.*) Fluther's
a friend o' mine, an' I'll not have him insulted.

The Covey (*struggling with the Barman*) Ay, leggo, leggo
there; fair hunt, give a man a fair hunt! One minute with
him is all I ask; one minute alone with him, while you're
runnin' for th' priest an' th' doctor.

Fluther (*to the Barman*) Let him go, let him go, Tom: let
him open th' door to sudden death if he wants to!

Barman (*to the Covey*) Go on, out you go an' do th' bowsey somewhere else. (*He pushes the Covey out and comes back.*)

Rosie (*getting Fluther's hat as he is putting on his coat*) Be God, you put th' fear o' God in his heart that time! I thought you'd have to be dug out of him . . . Th' way you lepped out without any of your fancy side-steppin'! 'Men like Fluther', say I to meself, 'is gettin' scarce nowadays.'

Fluther (*with proud complacency*) I wasn't goin' to let meself be malignified by a chancer . . . He got a little bit too derogatory for Fluther . . . Be God, to think of a cur like that comin' to talk to a man like me!

Rosie (*fixing on his hat*) Did j'ever!

Fluther He's lucky he got off safe. I hit a man last week, Rosie, an' he's fallin' yet!

Rosie Sure, you'd ha' broken him in two if you'd ha' hitten him one clatther!

Fluther (*amorously, putting his arm around Rosie*) Come on into th' snug, me little darlin', an' we'll have a few dhrinks before I see you home.

Rosie Oh, Fluther, I'm afraid you're a terrible man for th' women.

They go into the snug as Clitheroe, Captain Brennan, and Lieut. Langon of the Irish Volunteers enter hurriedly. Captain Brennan carries the banner of the Plough and the Stars, and Lieut. Langon a green, white and orange Tricolour. They are in a state of emotional excitement. Their faces are flushed and their eyes sparkle; they speak rapidly, as if unaware of the meaning of what they said. They have been mesmerized by the fervency of the speeches.

Clitheroe (*almost pantingly*) Three glasses o' port!

The Barman brings the drinks.

Capt. Brennan We won't have long to wait now.

Lieut. Langon Th' time is rotten ripe for revolution.

Clitheroe You have a mother, Langon.

Lieut. Langon Ireland is greater than a mother.

Capt. Brennan You have a wife, Clitheroe.

Clitheroe Ireland is greater than a wife.

Lieut. Langon Th' time for Ireland's battle is now – th' place for Ireland's battle is here.

The tall, dark figure again is silhouetted against the window. The three men pause and listen.

Voice of the Man Our foes are strong, but strong as they are, they cannot undo the miracles of God, who ripens in the heart of young men the seeds sown by the young men of a former generation. They think they have pacified Ireland; think they have foreseen everything; think they have provided against everything; but the fools, the fools, the fools! – they have left us our Fenian dead, and, while Ireland holds these graves, Ireland, unfree, shall never be at peace!

Capt. Brennan (*catching up the Plough and the Stars*) Imprisonment for th' Independence of Ireland!

Lieut. Langon (*catching up the Tricolour*) Wounds for th' Independence of Ireland!

Clitheroe Death for th' Independence of Ireland!

The Three (*together*) So help us God!

They drink. A bugle blows the Assembly. They hurry out. A pause. Fluther and Rosie come out of the snug;

Rosie is linking Fluther, who is a little drunk. Both are in a merry mood.

Rosie Come on home, ower o' that, man. Are you afraid or what? Are you goin' to come home, or are you not?

Fluther Of course I'm goin' home. What ud ail me that I wouldn't go?

Rosie (*lovingly*) Come on, then, oul' sport.

Officer's Voice (*giving command outside*) Irish Volunteers, by th' right, quick march!

Rosie (*putting her arm round Fluther and singing*)
I once had a lover, a tailor, but he could do nothin'
    for me,
An' then I fell in with a sailor as strong an' as wild
    as th' sea.
We cuddled an' kissed with devotion, till th' night
    from th' mornin' had fled;
An' there, to our joy, a bright bouncin' boy
Was dancin' a jig in th' bed!

Dancin' a jig in th' bed, an' bawlin' for butther an'
    bread.
An' there, to our joy, a bright bouncin' boy
Was dancin' a jig in th' bed!

They go out with their arms round each other.

Clitheroe's Voice (*in command outside*) Dublin Battalion of the Irish Citizen Army, by th' right, quick march!

Curtain.

Act Three

*The corner house in a street of tenements: it is the home
of the Clitheroes. The house is a long, gaunt, five-storey
tenement; its brick front is chipped and scarred with age
and neglect. The wide and heavy hall door, flanked by
two pillars, has a look of having been charred by a fire
in the distant past. The door lurches a little to one side,
disjointed by the continual and reckless banging when it
is being closed by most of the residents. The diamond-
paned fanlight is destitute of a single pane, the framework
alone remaining. The windows, except the two looking
into the front parlour (Clitheroe's room), are grimy, and
are draped with fluttering and soiled fragments of lace
curtains. The front parlour windows are hung with rich,
comparatively, casement cloth. Five stone steps lead from
the door to the path on the street. Branching on each
side are railings to prevent people from falling into the
area. At the left corner of the house runs a narrow lane,
bisecting the street, and connecting it with another of the
same kind. At the corner of the lane is a street lamp. As
the house is revealed, Mrs Gogan is seen helping Mollser
to a chair, which stands on the path beside the railings,
at the left side of the steps. She then wraps a shawl
around Mollser's shoulders. It is some months later.*

Mrs Gogan (*arranging shawl around Mollser*) Th' sun'll
do you all th' good in th' world. A few more weeks o'
this weather, an' there's no knowin' how well you'll be . . .
Are you comfy, now?

Mollser (*weakly and wearily*) Yis, ma; I'm all right.

Mrs Gogan How are you feelin'?

Mollser Betther, ma, betther. If th' horrible sinkin' feelin' ud go, I'd be all right.

Mrs Gogan Ah, I wouldn't put much pass on that. Your stomach maybe's out of ordher . . . Is th' poor breathin' any betther, d'ye think?

Mollser Yis, yis, ma; a lot betther.

Mrs Gogan Well, that's somethin' anyhow . . . With th' help o' God, you'll be on th' mend from this out . . . D'your legs feel any sthronger undher you, d'ye think?

Mollser (*irritably*) I can't tell, ma. I think so . . . A little.

Mrs Gogan Well, a little aself is somethin' . . . I thought I heard you coughin' a little more than usual last night . . . D'ye think you were?

Mollser I wasn't, ma, I wasn't.

Mrs Gogan I thought I heard you, for I was kep' awake all night with th' shootin'. An' thinkin' o' that madman, Fluther, runnin' about through th' night lookin' for Nora Clitheroe to bring her back when he heard she'd gone to folly her husband, an' in dhread any minute he might come staggerin' in covered with bandages, splashed all over with th' red of his own blood, an' givin' us barely time to bring th' priest to hear th' last whisper of his final confession, as his soul was passin' through th' dark doorway o' death into th' way o' th' wondherin' dead . . . You don't feel cold, do you?

Mollser No, ma; I'm all right.

Mrs Gogan Keep your chest well covered, for that's th' delicate spot in you . . . if there's any danger, I'll whip you in again . . . (*Looking up the street*) Oh, here's th' Covey an' oul' Pether hurryin' along. God Almighty, sthrange things is happenin' when them two is pullin' together.

The Covey and Peter come in, breathless and excited.

(*To the two men*) Were yous far up th' town? Did yous see any sign o' Fluther or Nora? How is things lookin'? I hear they're blazin' away out o' th' GPO. That th' Tommies is sthretched in heaps around Nelson's Pillar an' th' Parnell Statue, an' that th' pavin' sets in O'Connell Street is nearly covered be pools o' blood.

Peter We seen no sign o' Nora or Fluther anywhere.

Mrs Gogan We should ha' held her back be main force from goin' to look for her husband . . . God knows what's happened to her – I'm always seein' her sthretched on her back in some hospital, moanin' with th' pain of a bullet in her vitals, an' nuns thryin' to get her to take a last look at th' crucifix!

The Covey We can do nothin'. You can't stick your nose into O'Connell Street, an' Tyler's is on fire.

Peter An' we seen th' Lancers –

The Covey (*interrupting*) Throttin' along, heads in th' air; spurs an' sabres jinglin', an' lances quiverin', an' lookin' as if they were assin' themselves, 'Where's these blighters, till we get a prod at them?' when there was a volley from th' Post Office that stretched half o' them, an' sent th' rest gallopin' away wondherin' how far they'd have to go before they'd feel safe.

Peter (*rubbing his hands*) 'Damn it,' says I to meself, 'this looks like business!'

The Covey An' then out comes General Pearse an' his staff, an', standin' in th' middle o' th' street, he reads th' Proclamation.

Mrs Gogan What proclamation?

Peter Declarin' an Irish Republic.

Mrs Gogan Go to God!

Peter The gunboat *Helga*'s shellin' Liberty Hall, an' I hear the people livin' on th' quays had to crawl on their bellies to Mass with th' bullets that were flyin' around from Boland's Mills.

Mrs Gogan God bless us, what's goin' to be th' end of it all!

Bessie (*looking out of the top window*) Maybe yous are satisfied now; maybe yous are satisfied now. Go on an' get guns if yous are men – Johnny get your gun, get your gun, get your gun! Yous are all nicely shanghaied now; th' boyo hasn't a sword on his thigh now! Oh, yous are all nicely shanghaied now!

Mrs Gogan (*warningly to Peter and the Covey*) S-s-sh, don't answer her. She's th' right oul' Orange bitch! She's been chantin' 'Rule, Britannia' all th' mornin'.

Peter I hope Fluther hasn't met with any accident, he's such a wild card.

Mrs Gogan God grant it; but last night I dreamt I seen gettin' carried into th' house a sthretcher with a figure lyin' on it, stiff an' still, dhressed in th' habit of Saint Francis. An, then, I heard th' murmurs of a crowd no one could see sayin' th' litany for th' dead; an' then it got so dark that nothin' was seen but th' white face of th' corpse, gleamin' like a white wather-lily floatin' on th' top of a dark lake. Then a tiny whisper thrickled into me ear, sayin', 'Isn't the face very like th' face o' Fluther?' an' then, with a thremblin' flutther, th' dead lips opened, an', although I couldn't hear, I knew they were sayin', 'Poor oul' Fluther, afther havin' handed in his gun at last, his shakin' soul moored in th' place where th' wicked are at rest an' th' weary cease from throublin'.'

Peter (*who has put on a pair of spectacles, and has been looking down the street*) Here they are, be God, here they are; just afther turnin' th' corner – Nora an' Fluther!

The Covey She must be wounded or something – he seems to be carryin' her.

Fluther and Nora enter. Fluther has his arm around her and is half-leading, half-carrying her in. Her eyes are dim and hollow, her face pale and strained-looking; her hair is tossed, and her clothes are dusty.

Mrs Gogan (*running over to them*) God bless us, is it wounded y'are, Mrs Clitheroe, or what?

Fluther Ah, she's all right, Mrs Gogan; only worn out from thravellin' an' want o'sleep. A night's rest, now, an' she'll be as fit as a fiddle. Bring her in, an' make her lie down.

Mrs Gogan (*to Nora*) Did you hear e'er a whisper o' Mr Clitheroe?

Nora (*wearily*) I could find him nowhere, Mrs Gogan. None o' them would tell me where he was. They told me I shamed my husband an' th' women of Ireland be carryin' on as I was . . . They said th' women must learn to be brave an' cease to be cowardly . . . Me who risked more for love than they would risk for hate . . . (*Raising her voice in hysterical protest*) My Jack will be killed, my Jack will be killed! . . . He is to be butchered as a sacrifice to th' dead!

Bessie (*from upper window*) Yous are all nicely shanghaied now! Sorra mend th' lasses that have been kissin' an' cuddlin' their boys into th' sheddin' of blood! . . . Fillin' their minds with fairy tales that had no beginnin', but, please God, 'll have a bloody quick endin'! . . . Turnin' bitther into sweet, an' sweet into bitther . . . Stabbin' in th' back th' men that are dyin' in th' threnches for them! It's a bad thing for anyone that thries to jilt th' Ten Commandments, for judgements are prepared for scorners an' sthripes for th' back o' fools! (*Going away from window as she sings*)

Rule, Britannia, Britannia rules th' waves,
Britons never, never, never shall be slaves!

Fluther (*with a roar up at the window*) Y'ignorant oul' throllope, you!

Mrs Gogan (*to Nora*) He'll come home safe enough to you, you'll find, Mrs Clitheroe; afther all, there's a power o' women that's handed over sons an' husbands to take a runnin' risk in th' fight they're wagin'.

Nora I can't help thinkin' every shot fired 'll be fired at Jack, an' every shot fired at Jack'll be fired at me. What do I care for th' others? I can think only of me own self . . . An' there's no woman gives a son or a husband to be killed – if they say it, they're lyin', lyin', against God, Nature, an' against themselves! . . . One blasted hussy at a barricade told me to go home an' not be thryin' to dishearten th' men . . . That I wasn't worthy to bear a son to a man that was out fightin' for freedom . . . I clawed at her, an' smashed her in th' face till we were separated . . . I was pushed down th' street, an' I cursed them – cursed the rebel ruffians an' Volunteers that had dhragged me ravin' mad into th' sthreets to seek me husband!

Peter You'll have to have patience, Nora. We all have to put up with twarthers an' tormentors in this world.

The Covey If they were fightin' for anything worth while, I wouldn't mind.

Fluther (*to Nora*) Nothin' derogatory 'll happen to Mr Clitheroe. You'll find, now, in th' finish up it'll be vice versa.

Nora Oh, I know that wherever he is, he's thinkin' of wantin' to be with me. I know he's longin' to be passin' his hand through me hair, to be caressin' me neck, to fondle me hand an' to feel me kisses clingin' to his mouth . . . An' he stands wherever he is because he's brave? (*Vehemently*) No, but because he's a coward, a coward, a coward!

Mrs Gogan Oh, they're not cowards anyway.

Nora (*with denunciatory anger*) I tell you they're afraid to say they're afraid! . . . Oh, I saw it, I saw it, Mrs Gogan . . . At th' barricade in North King Street I saw fear glowin' in all their eyes . . . An' in th' middle o' th' sthreet was somethin' huddled up in a horrible, tangled heap . . . His face was jammed again th' stones, an' his arm was twisted round his back . . . An' every twist of his body was a cry against th' terrible thing that had happened to him . . . An' I saw they were afraid to look at it . . . An' some o' them laughed at me, but th' laugh was a frightened one . . . An' some o' them shouted at me, but th' shout had in it th' shiver o' fear . . . I tell you they were afraid, afraid, afraid!

Mrs Gogan (*leading her towards the house*) Come on in, dear. If you'd been a little longer together, th' wrench asundher wouldn't have been so sharp.

Nora Th' agony I'm in since he left me has thrust away every rough thing he done, an' every unkind word he spoke; only th' blossoms that grew out of our lives are before me now; shakin' their colours before me face, an' breathin' their sweet scent on every thought springin' up in me mind, till, sometimes, Mrs Gogan, sometimes I think I'm goin' mad!

Mrs Gogan You'll be a lot betther when you have a little lie down.

Nora (*turning towards Fluther as she is going in*) I don't know what I'd have done, only for Fluther. I'd have been lyin' in th' streets, only for him . . . (*As she goes in*) They have dhriven away th' little happiness life had to spare for me. He has gone from me for ever, for ever . . . Oh, Jack, Jack, Jack!

> *She is led in by Mrs Gogan as Bessie comes out with a shawl around her shoulders. She passes by them with her head in the air. When they have gone in, she gives a mug of milk to Mollser silently.*

Fluther Which of yous has th' tossers?

The Covey I have.

Bessie (*as she is passing them to go down the street*) You an' your Leadhers an' their sham-battle soldiers has landed a body in a nice way, havin' to go an' ferret out a bit o' bread God knows where . . . Why aren't yous in th' GPO if yous are men? It's paler an' paler yous are gettin' . . . A lot o' vipers, that's what th' Irish people is! (*She goes out.*)

Fluther Never mind her . . . (*To the Covey*) Make a start an' keep us from th' sin o' idleness. (*To Mollser*) Well, how are you today, Mollser, oul' son? What are you dhrinkin', milk?

Mollser Grand, Fluther, grand, thanks. Yis, milk.

Fluther You couldn't get a betther thing down you . . . This turn-up has done one good thing, anyhow; you can't get dhrink anywhere, an' if it lasts a week, I'll be so used to it that I won't think of a pint.

The Covey (*who has taken from his pocket two worn coins and a thin strip of wood about four inches long*) What's th' bettin'?

Peter Heads, a juice.

Fluther Harps, a tanner.

The Covey places the coins on the strip of wood, and flips them up into the air. As they jingle on the ground the distant boom of a big gun is heard. They stand for a moment listening.

What th' hell's that?

The Covey It's like th' boom of a big gun!

Fluther Surely to God they're not goin' to use artillery on us?

The Covey (*scornfully*) Not goin'! (*Vehemently*) Wouldn't they use anything on us, man?

Fluther Aw, holy Christ, that's not playin' th' game!

Peter (*plaintively*) What would happen if a shell landed here now?

The Covey (*ironically*) You'd be off to heaven in a fiery chariot.

Peter In spite of all th' warnin's that's ringin' around us, are you goin' to start your pickin' at me again?

Fluther Go on, toss them again, toss them again . . . Harps, a tanner.

Peter Heads, a juice.

The Covey tosses the coins.

Fluther (*as the coins fall*) Let them roll, let them roll. Heads, be God!

Bessie runs in excitedly. She has a new hat on her head, a fox fur round her neck over her shawl, three umbrellas under her right arm, and a box of biscuits under her left. She speaks rapidly and breathlessly.

Bessie They're breakin' into th' shops, they're breakin' into th' shops! Smashin' th' windows, battherin' in th' doors, an' whippin' away everything! An' th' Volunteers is firin' on them. I seen two men an' a lassie pushin' a piano down th' sthreet, an' th' sweat rollin' off them thryin' to get it up on th' pavement; an' an oul' wan that must ha' been seventy lookin' as if she'd dhrop every minute with th' dint o' heart beatin', thryin' to pull a big double bed out of a broken shop-window! I was goin' to wait till I dhressed meself from th' skin out.

Mollser (*to Bessie, as she is going in*) Help me in, Bessie; I'm feelin' curious.

Bessie leaves the looted things in the house, and, rapidly returning, helps Mollser in.

The Covey Th' selfishness of that one – she waited till she got all she could carry before she'd come to tell anyone!

Fluther (*running over to the door of the house and shouting in to Bessie*) Ay, Bessie, did you hear of e'er a pub gettin' a shake up?

Bessie (*inside*) I didn't hear o' none.

Fluther (*in a burst of enthusiasm*) Well, you're goin' to hear of one soon!

The Covey Come on, man, an' don't be wastin' time.

Peter (*to them as they are about to run off*) Ay, ay, are you goin' to leave me here?

Fluther Are you goin' to leave yourself here?

Peter (*anxiously*) Didn't yous hear her sayin' they were firin' on them?

The Covey *and* **Fluther** (*together*) Well?

Peter Supposin' I happened to be potted?

Fluther We'd give you a Christian burial, anyhow.

The Covey (*ironically*) Dhressed up in your regimentals.

Peter (*to the Covey, passionately*) May th' all-lovin' God give you a hot knock one o' these days, me young Covey, tuthorin' Fluther up now to be tiltin' at me, an' crossin' me with his mockeries an' jibin'!

A fashionably dressed, middle-aged, stout woman comes hurriedly in, and makes for the group. She is almost fainting with fear.

Woman For Gawd's sake, will one of you kind men show any safe way for me to get to Wrathmines? . . . I was foolish enough to visit a friend, thinking the howl thing was a joke, and now I cawn't get a car or a tram to take me home – isn't it awful? ·

Fluther I'm afraid, ma'am, one way is as safe as another.

Woman And what am I gowing to do? Oh, isn't this awful? . . . I'm so different from others . . . The mowment I hear a shot, my legs give way under me – I cawn't stir, I'm paralysed – isn't it awful?

Fluther (*moving away*) It's a derogatory way to be, right enough, ma'am.

Woman (*catching Fluther's coat*) Creeping along the street there, with my head down and my eyes half shut, a bullet whizzed past within an inch of my nowse . . . I had to lean against the wall for a long time, gasping

for breath – I nearly passed away – it was awful! . . .
I wonder, would you kind men come some of the way
and see me safe?

Fluther I have to go away, ma'am, to thry an' save a few
things from th' burnin' buildin's.

The Covey Come on, then, or there won't be anything
left to save.

The Covey and Fluther hurry away.

Woman (*to Peter*) Wasn't it an awful thing for me to
leave my friend's house? Wasn't it an idiotic thing to
do? . . . I haven't the slightest idea where I am . . . You
have a kind face, sir. Could you possibly come and pilot
me in the direction of Wrathmines?

Peter (*indignantly*) D'ye think I'm goin' to risk me life
throttin' in front of you? An' maybe get a bullet that
would gimme a game leg or something that would leave
me a jibe an' a jeer to Fluther an' th' young Covey for
th' rest o' me days! (*With an indignant toss of his head
he walks into the house.*)

Woman (*going out*) I know I'll fall down in a dead faint
if I hear another shot go off anyway near me – isn't it
awful!

*Mrs Gogan comes out of the house pushing a pram
before her. As she enters the street, Bessie rushes out,
follows Mrs Gogan, and catches hold of the pram,
stopping Mrs Gogan's progress.*

Bessie Here, where are you goin' with that? How quick
you were, me lady, to clap your eyes on th' pram . . .
Maybe you don't know that Mrs Sullivan, before she
went to spend Easther with her people in Dunboyne,
gave me sthrict injunctions to give an accasional look to
see if it was still standin' where it was left in th' corner
of th' lobby.

66

Mrs Gogan That remark of yours, Mrs Bessie Burgess, requires a little considheration, seein' that th' pram was left on our lobby, an' not on yours; a foot or two a little to th' left of th' jamb of me own room door; nor is it needful to mention th' name of th' person that gave a squint to see if it was there th' first thing in th' mornin', an' th' last thing in th' stillness o' th' night; never failin' to realize that her eyes couldn't be goin' wrong, be sthretchin' out her arm an' runnin' her hand over th' pram, to make sure that th' sight was no deception! Moreover, somethin's tellin' me that th' runnin' hurry of an inthrest you're takin' in it now is a sudden ambition to use th' pram for a purpose that a loyal woman of law an' ordher would stagger away from! (*She gives the pram a sudden push that pulls Bessie forward.*)

Bessie (*still holding the pram*) There's not as much as one body in th' house that doesn't know that it wasn't Bessie Burgess that was always shakin' her voice complainin' about people leavin' bassinettes in th' way of them that, week in an' week out, had to pay their rent, an' always had to find a regular accommodation for her own furniture in her own room . . . An' as for law an' ordher, puttin' aside th' harp an' shamrock, Bessie Burgess 'll have as much respect as she wants for th' lion an' unicorn!

Peter (*appearing at the door*) I think I'll go with th' pair of yous an' see th' fun. A fella might as well chance it, anyhow.

Mrs Gogan (*taking no notice of Peter, and pushing the pram on another step*) Take your rovin' lumps o' hands from pattin' th' bassinette, if you please, ma'am; an', steppin' from th' threshold of good manners, let me tell you, Mrs Burgess, that's it's a fat wondher to Jennie Gogan that a lady-like singer o' hymns like yourself would lower her thoughts from sky-thinkin' to sthretch out her arm in a sly-seekin' way to pinch anything dhriven asthray in th' confusion of th' battle our boys is makin' for th' freedom of their counthry!

Peter (*laughing and rubbing his hands together*) Hee, hee, hee, hee, hee! I'll go with th' pair o' yous an' give yous a hand.

Mrs Gogan (*with a rapid turn of her head as she shoves the pram forward*) Get up in th' prambulator an' we'll wheel you down.

Bessie (*to Mrs Gogan*) Poverty an' hardship has sent Bessie Burgess to abide with sthrange company, but she always knew them she had to live with from backside to breakfast time; an' she can tell them, always havin' had a Christian kinch on her conscience, that a passion for thievin' an' pinchin' would find her soul a foreign place to live in, an' that her present intention is quite th' lofty-hearted one of pickin' up anything shaken up an' scatthered about in th' loose confusion of a general plundher!

By this time they have disappeared from view. Peter is following, when the boom of a big gun in the distance brings him to a quick halt.

Peter God Almighty, that's th' big gun again! God forbid any harm would happen to them, but sorra mind I'd mind if they met with a dhrop in their mad endeyvours to plundher an' desthroy.

He looks down the street for a moment, then runs to the hall door of the house, which is open, and shuts it with a vicious pull; he then goes to the chair in which Mollser had sat, sits down, takes out his pipe, lights it and begins to smoke with his head carried at a haughty angle. The Covey comes staggering in with a

68

ten-stone sack of flour on his back. On the top of the sack is a ham. He goes over to the door, pushes it with his head, and finds he can't open it; he turns slightly in the direction of Peter.

The Covey (*to Peter*) Who shut th' door? . . . (*He kicks at it.*) Here, come on an' open it, will you? This isn't a mot's hand-bag I've got on me back.

Peter Now, me young Covey, d'ye think I'm goin' to be your lackey?

The Covey (*angrily*) Will you open th' door, y'oul' –

Peter (*shouting*) Don't be assin' me to open any door, don't be assin' me to open any door for you . . . Makin' a shame an' a sin o' th' cause that good men are fightin' for . . . Oh, God forgive th' people that, instead o' burnishin' th' work th' boys is doin' today with quiet honesty an' patience, is revilin' their sacrifices with a riot of lootin' an' roguery!

The Covey Isn't your own eyes leppin' out o' your head with envy that you haven't th' guts to ketch a few o' th' things that God is givin' to His chosen people? . . . Y'oul' hypocrite, if everyone was blind you'd steal a cross off an ass's back!

Peter (*very calmly*) You're not going to make me lose me temper; you can go on with your proddin' as long as you like; goad an' goad an' goad away; hee, hee, heee! I'll not lose me temper.

Somebody opens door and the Covey goes in.

The Covey (*inside, mockingly*) Cuckoo-oo!

Peter (*running to the door and shouting in a blaze of passion as he follows the Covey in*) You lean, long, lanky lath of a lowsey bastard . . . (*Following him in*) Lowsey bastard, lowsey bastard!

69

Bessie and Mrs Gogan enter, the pride of a great joy illuminating their faces. Bessie is pushing the pram, which is filled with clothes and boots; on the top of the boots and clothes is a fancy table, which Mrs Gogan is holding on with her left hand, while with her right hand she holds a chair on the top of her head. They are heard talking to each other before they enter.

Mrs Gogan (*outside*) I don't remember ever havin' seen such lovely pairs as them, (*they appear*) with th' pointed toes an' th' cuban heels.

Bessie They'll go grand with th' dhresses we're afther liftin', when we've stitched a sthray bit o' silk to lift th' bodices up a little bit higher, so as to shake th' shame out o' them, an' make them fit for women that hasn't lost themselves in th' nakedness o' th' times.

They fussily carry in the chair, the table, and some of the other goods. They return to bring in the rest.

Peter (*at door, sourly to Mrs Gogan*) Ay, you. Mollser looks as if she was goin' to faint, an' your youngster is roarin' in convulsions in her lap.

Mrs Gogan (*snappily*) She's never any other way but faintin'!

She goes to go in with some things in her arms, when a shot from a rifle rings out. She and Bessie make a bolt for the door, which Peter, in a panic, tries to shut before they have got inside.

Ay, ay, ay, you cowardly oul' fool, what are you thryin' to shut th' door on us for?

They retreat tumultuously inside. A pause; then Captain Brennan comes in supporting Lieutenant Langon, whose arm is around Brennan's neck.

Langon's face, which is ghastly white, is momentarily convulsed with spasms of agony. He is in a state of collapse, and Brennan is almost carrying him. After a few moments Clitheroe, pale, and in a state of calm nervousness, follows, looking back in the direction from which he came, a rifle, held at the ready, in his hands.

Capt. Brennan (*savagely to Clitheroe*) Why did you fire over their heads? Why didn't you fire to kill?

Clitheroe No, no, Bill; bad as they are they're Irish men an' women.

Capt. Brennan (*savagely*) Irish be damned! Attackin' an' mobbin' th' men that are riskin' their lives for them. If these slum lice gather at our heels again, plug one o' them, or I'll soon shock them with a shot or two meself!

Lieut. Langon (*moaningly*) My God, is there ne'er an ambulance knockin' around anywhere? . . . Th' stomach is ripped out o' me; I feel it – o-o-oh, Christ!

Capt. Brennan Keep th' heart up, Jim; we'll soon get help, now.

Nora rushes wildly out of the house and flings her arms round the neck of Clitheroe with a fierce and joyous insistence. Her hair is down, her face is haggard, but her eyes are agleam with the light of happy relief

Nora Jack, Jack, Jack; God be thanked . . . be thanked . . . He has been kind and merciful to His poor handmaiden . . . My Jack, my own Jack, that I thought was lost is found, that I thought was dead is alive again! . . . Oh, God be praised for ever, evermore! . . . My poor Jack . . . Kiss me, kiss me, Jack, kiss your own Nora!

Clitheroe (*kissing her, and speaking brokenly*) My Nora; my little, beautiful Nora, I wish to God I'd never left you.

Nora It doesn't matter – not now, not now, Jack. It will make us dearer than ever to each other . . . Kiss me, kiss me again.

Clitheroe Now, for God's sake, Nora, don't make a scene.

Nora I won't, I won't; I promise, I promise, Jack; honest to God. I'll be silent an' brave to bear th' joy of feelin' you safe in my arms again . . . It's hard to force away th' tears of happiness at th' end of an awful agony.

Bessie (*from the upper window*) Th' Minsthrel Boys aren't feelin' very comfortable now. Th' big guns has knocked all th' harps out of their hands. General Clitheroe'd rather be unlacin' his wife's bodice than standin' at a barricade . . . An' th' professor of chicken-butcherin' there, finds he's up against somethin' a little tougher even than his own chickens, an' that's sayin' a lot!

Capt. Brennan (*up to Bessie*) Shut up, y'oul' hag!

Bessie (*down to Brennan*) Choke th' chicken, choke th' chicken, choke th' chicken!

Lieut. Langon For God's sake, Bill, bring me some place where me wound 'll be looked afther . . . Am I to die before anything is done to save me?

Capt. Brennan (*to Clitheroe*) Come on, Jack. We've got to get help for Jim, here – have you no thought for his pain an' danger?

Bessie Choke th' chicken, choke th' chicken, choke th' chicken!

Clitheroe (*to Nora*) Loosen me, darling, let me go.

Nora (*clinging to him*) No, no, no, I'll not let you go!
Come on, come up to our home, Jack, my sweetheart,
my lover, my husband, an' we'll forget th' last few
terrible days! . . . I look tired now, but a few hours of
happy rest in your arms will bring back th' bloom of
freshness again, an' you will be glad, you will be glad,
glad . . . glad!

Lieut. Langon Oh, if I'd kep' down only a little longer,
I mightn't ha' been hit! Everyone else escapin', an' me
gettin' me belly ripped asundher! . . . I couldn't scream,
couldn't even scream . . . D'ye think I'm really badly
wounded, Bill? Me clothes seem to be all soakin' wet . . .
It's blood . . . My God, it must be me own blood!

Capt. Brennan (*to Clitheroe*) Go on, Jack, bid her
goodbye with another kiss, an' be done with it! D'ye
want Langon to die in me arms while you're dallyin'
with your Nora?

Clitheroe (*to Nora*) I must go, I must go, Nora. I'm
sorry we met at all . . . It couldn't be helped – all other
ways were blocked be th' British . . . Let me go, can't you,
Nora? D'ye want me to be unthrue to me comrades?

Nora No, I won't let you go . . . I want you to be thrue
to me, Jack . . . I'm your dearest comrade; I'm your
thruest comrade . . . They only want th' comfort of havin'
you in th' same danger as themselves . . . Oh, Jack,
I can't let you go!

Clitheroe You must, Nora, you must.

Nora All last night at th' barricades I sought you,
Jack . . . I didn't think of th' danger – I could only think
of you . . . I asked for you everywhere . . . Some o' them
laughed . . . I was pushed away, but I shoved back . . .
Some o' them even sthruck me . . . an' I screamed an'
screamed your name!

Clitheroe (*in fear her action would give him future shame*) What possessed you to make a show of yourself, like that? . . . What way d'ye think I'll feel when I'm told my wife was bawlin' for me at th' barricades? What are you more than any other woman?

Nora No more, maybe; but you are more to me than any other man, Jack . . . I didn't mean any harm, honestly, Jack . . . I couldn't help it . . . I shouldn't have told you . . . My love for you made me mad with terror.

Clitheroe (*angrily*) They'll say now that I sent you out th' way I'd have an excuse to bring you home . . . Are you goin' to turn all th' risks I'm takin' into a laugh?

Lieut. Langon Let me lie down, let me lie down, Bill; th' pain would be easier, maybe, lyin' down . . . Oh, God, have mercy on me!

Capt. Brennan (*to Langon*) A few steps more, Jim, a few steps more; thry to stick it for a few steps more.

Lieut. Langon Oh, I can't, I can't, I can't!

Capt. Brennan (*to Clitheroe*) Are you comin', man, or are you goin' to make an arrangement for another honeymoon? . . . If you want to act th' renegade, say so, an' we'll be off!

Bessie (*from above*) Runnin' from th' Tommies – choke th' chicken. Runnin' from th' Tommies – choke th' chicken!

Clitheroe (*savagely to Brennan*) Damn you, man, who wants to act th' renegade? (*to Nora*) Here, let go your hold; let go, I say!

Nora (*clinging to Clitheroe, and indicating Brennan*) Look, Jack, look at th' anger in his face; look at th' fear glintin' in his eyes . . . He himself's afraid, afraid, afraid! . . . He wants you to go th' way he'll have

74

th' chance of death sthrikin' you an' missin' him! . . . Turn round an' look at him, Jack, look at him, look at him! . . . His very soul is cold . . . shiverin' with th' thought of what may happen to him . . . It is his fear that is thryin' to frighten you from recognizin' th' same fear that is in your own heart!

Clitheroe (*struggling to release himself from Nora*) Damn you, woman, will you let me go!

Capt. Brennan (*fiercely, to Clitheroe*) Why are you beggin' her to let you go? Are you afraid of her, or what? Break her hold on you, man, or go up, an' sit on her lap!

Clitheroe tries roughly to break Nora's hold.

Nora (*imploringly*) Oh, Jack . . . Jack . . . Jack!

Lieut. Langon (*agonizingly*) Brennan, a priest; I'm dyin', I think, I'm dyin'!

Clitheroe (*to Nora*) If you won't do it quietly, I'll have to make you! (*To Brennan*) Here, hold this gun, you, for a minute. (*He hands the gun to Brennan.*)

Nora (*pitifully*) Please, Jack . . . You're hurting me, Jack . . . Honestly . . . Oh, you're hurting . . . me! . . . I won't, I won't, I won't! . . . Oh, Jack, I gave you everything you asked of me . . . Don't fling me from you, now!

Clitheroe roughly loosens her grip, and pushes her away from him. Nora sinks to the ground and lies there.

(*Weakly*) Ah, Jack . . . Jack . . . Jack!

Clitheroe (*taking the gun back from Brennan*) Come on, come on.

They go out. Bessie looks at Nora lying on the street, for a few moments, then, leaving the window, she

75

comes out, runs over to Nora, lifts her up in her arms, and carries her swiftly into the house. A short pause, then down the street is heard a wild, drunken yell; it comes nearer, and Fluther enters, frenzied, wild-eyed, mad, roaring drunk. In his arms is an earthen half-gallon jar of whiskey; streaming from one of the pockets of his coat is the arm of a new tunic shirt; on his head is a woman's vivid blue hat with gold lacing, all of which he has looted.

Fluther (*singing in a frenzy*)
Fluther's a jolly good fella! . . . Fluther's a jolly good fella!
Up th' rebels! . . . That nobody can deny!

(*He beats on the door.*) Get us a mug or a jug, or somethin', some o' yous, one o' yous, will yous, before I lay one o' yous out! . . . (*Looking down the street*) Bang an' fire away for all Fluther cares . . . (*Banging at door*) Come down an' open th' door, some of yous, one o' yous, will yous, before I lay some o' yous out! . . . Th' whole city can topple home to hell, for Fluther!

Inside the house is heard a scream from Nora, followed by a moan.

Fluther (*singing furiously*)
That nobody can deny, that nobody can deny,
For Fluther's a jolly good fella, Fluther's a jolly good fella,
Fluther's a jolly good fella . . . Up th' rebels! That nobody can deny!

(*His frantic movements cause him to spill some of the whiskey out of the jar.*) Blast you, Fluther, don't be spillin' th' precious liquor! (*He kicks at the door.*) Ay, give us a mug or a jug or somethin', one o' yous, some o' yous, will yous, before I lay one o' yous out!

The door suddenly opens, and Bessie, coming out, grips him by the collar.

Bessie (*indignantly*) You bowsey, come in ower o' that . . . I'll thrim your thricks o' dhrunken dancin' for you, an' none of us knowin' how soon we'll bump into a world we were never in before!

Fluther (*as she is pulling him in*) Ay, th' jar, th' jar, th' jar!

A short pause, then again is heard a scream of pain from Nora. The door opens and Mrs Gogan and Bessie are seen standing at it.

Bessie Fluther would go, only he's too dhrunk . . . Oh, God, isn't it a pity he's so dhrunk! We'll have to thry to get a docthor somewhere.

Mrs Gogan I'd be afraid to go . . . Besides, Mollser's terrible bad. I don't think you'll get a docthor to come. It's hardly any use goin'.

Bessie (*determinedly*) I'll risk it . . . Give her a little of Fluther's whiskey . . . It's th' fright that's brought it on her so soon . . . Go on back to her, you.

Mrs Gogan goes in, and Bessie softly closes the door. She is moving forward, when the sound of some rifle shots, and the tok, tok, tok of a distant machine-gun bring her to a sudden halt. She hesitates for a moment, then she tightens her shawl round her, as if it were a shield, then she firmly and swiftly goes out.

(*As she goes out*) Oh, God, be Thou my help in time o' throuble. An' shelter me safely in th' shadow of Thy wings!

Curtain.

Act Four

The living-room of Bessie Burgess. It is one of two small attic rooms (the other, used as a bedroom, is to the left), the ceiling slopes up towards the back, giving to the apartment a look of compressed confinement. In the centre of the ceiling is a small skylight. There is an unmistakable air of poverty bordering on destitution. The paper on the walls is torn and soiled, particularly near the fire where the cooking is done, and near the washstand where the washing is done. The fireplace is to the left. A small armchair near fire. One small window at back. A pane of this window is starred by the entrance of a bullet. Under the window to the right is an oak coffin standing on two kitchen chairs. Near the coffin is a home-manufactured stool, on which are two lighted candles. Beside the window is a worn-out dresser on which is a small quantity of delft. Tattered remains of cheap lace curtains drape the window. Standing near the window on left is a brass standard-lamp with a fancy shade; hanging on the wall near the same window is a vividly crimson silk dress, both of which have been looted. A door on left leading to the bedroom. Another opposite giving a way to the rest of the house. To the left of this door a common washstand. A tin kettle, very black, and an old saucepan inside the fender. There is no light in the room but that given from the two candles and the fire. The dusk has well fallen, and the glare of the burning buildings in the town can be seen through the window, in the distant sky. The Covey and Fluther have been playing cards, sitting on the floor by the light of the candles on the stool near the coffin.

78

*When the curtain rises the Covey is shuffling the cards,
Peter is sitting in a stiff, dignified way beside him, and
Fluther is kneeling beside the window, cautiously looking
out. It is a few days later.*

Fluther (*furtively peeping out of the window*) Give them
a good shuffling . . . Th' sky's gettin' reddher an' reddher
. . . You'd think it was afire . . . Half o' th' city must be
burnin'.

The Covey If I was you, Fluther, I'd keep away from
that window . . . It's dangerous, an' besides, if they see
you, you'll only bring a nose on th' house.

Peter Yes; an' he knows we had to leave our own place
th' way they were riddlin' it with machine-gun fire . . .
He'll keep on pimpin' and pimpin' there, till we have to
fly out o' this place too.

Fluther (*ironically*) If they make any attack here, we'll
send you out in your green an' glory uniform, shakin'
your sword over your head, an' they'll fly before you as
th' Danes flew before Brian Boru!

The Covey (*placing the cards on the floor, after shuffling
them*) Come on, an' cut.

Fluther comes over, sits on floor, and cuts the cards.

(*Having dealt the cards*) Spuds up again.

Nora moans feebly in room on left.

Fluther There, she's at it again. She's been quiet for a
long time, all th' same.

The Covey She was quiet before, sure, an' she broke out
again worse than ever . . . What was led that time?

Peter Thray o' Hearts, Thray o' Hearts, Thray o' Hearts.

Fluther It's damned hard lines to think of her dead-born kiddie lyin' there in th' arms o' poor little Mollser. Mollser snuffed it sudden too, afther all.

The Covey Sure she never got any care. How could she get it, an' th' mother out day an' night lookin' for work, an' her consumptive husband leavin' her with a baby to be born before he died!

Voices (*in a lilting chant to the left in a distant street*) Red Cr . . . oss, Red Cr . . . oss! . . . Ambu . . . lance, Ambu . . . lance!

The Covey (*to Fluther*) Your deal, Fluther.

Fluther (*shuffling and dealing the cards*) It'll take a lot out o' Nora – if she'll ever be th' same.

The Covey The docthor thinks she'll never be th' same; thinks she'll be a little touched here. (*He touches his forehead.*) She's ramblin' a lot; thinkin' she's out in th' counthry with Jack; or gettin' his dinner ready for him before he comes home; or yellin' for her kiddie. All that, though, might be th' chloroform she got . . . I don't know what we'd have done only for oul' Bessie; up with her for th' past three nights, hand runnin'.

Fluther I always knew there was never anything really derogatory wrong with poor oul' Bessie. (*To Peter, who is taking a trick*) Ay, houl' on, there, don't be so damn quick – that's my thrick.

Peter What's your thrick? It's my thrick, man.

Fluther (*loudly*) How is it your thrick?

Peter (*answering as loudly*) Didn't I lead th' deuce!

Fluther You must be gettin' blind, man; don't you see th' ace?

Bessie (*appearing at door of room, left; in a tense whisper*) D'ye want to waken her again on me, when she's just gone asleep? If she wakes will yous come an' mind her? If I hear a whisper out o' one o' yous again, I'll gut yous!

The Covey (*in a whisper*) S-s-s-h. She can hear anything above a whisper.

Peter (*looking up at the ceiling*) Th' gentle an' merciful God 'll give th' pair o' yous a scawldin' an' a scarifyin' one o' these days!

Fluther takes a bottle of whiskey from his pocket, and takes a drink.

The Covey (*to Fluther*) Why don't you spread that out, man, an' thry to keep a sup for tomorrow?

Fluther Spread it out? Keep a sup for tomorrow? How th' hell does a fella know there'll be any tomorrow? If I'm goin' to be whipped away, let me be whipped away when it's empty, an' not when it's half full! (*To Bessie, who has seated herself in an armchair at the fire*) How is she, now, Bessie?

Bessie I left her sleeping quietly. When I'm listenin' to her babblin', I think she'll never be much betther than she is. Her eyes have a hauntin' way of lookin' in instead of lookin' out, as if her mind had been lost alive in madly minglin' memories of th' past . . . (*Sleepily*) Crushin' her thoughts . . . together . . . in a fierce . . . an' fanciful . . . (*she nods her head and starts wakefully*) idea that dead things are livin', an' livin' things are dead . . . (*With a start*) Was that a scream I heard her give? (*Reassured*) Blessed God, I think I hear her screamin' every minute! An' it's only there with me that I'm able to keep awake.

The Covey She'll sleep, maybe, for a long time, now. Ten there.

Fluther Ten here. If she gets a long sleep, she might be all right. Peter's th' lone five.

The Covey Whisht! I think I hear somebody movin' below. Whoever it is, he's comin' up.

A pause. Then the door opens and Captain Brennan comes into the room. He has changed his uniform for a suit of civvies. His eyes droop with the heaviness of exhaustion; his face is pallid and drawn. His clothes are dusty and stained here and there with mud. He leans heavily on the back of a chair as he stands.

Capt. Brennan Mrs Clitheroe; where's Mrs Clitheroe? I was told I'd find her here.

Bessie What d'ye want with Mrs Clitheroe?

Capt. Brennan I've a message, a last message for her from her husband.

Bessie Killed! He's not killed, is he!

Capt. Brennan (*sinking stiffly and painfully on to a chair*) In th' Imperial Hotel; we fought till th' place was in flames. He was shot through th' arm, an' then through th' lung . . . I could do nothin' for him – only watch his breath comin' an' goin' in quick, jerky gasps, an' a tiny sthream o' blood thricklin' out of his mouth, down over his lower lip . . . I said a prayer for th' dyin', an' twined his Rosary beads around his fingers . . . Then I had to leave him to save meself . . . (*He shows some holes in his coat.*) Look at th' way a machine-gun tore at me coat, as I belted out o' th' buildin' an' darted across th' sthreet for shelter . . . An' then, I seen the Plough an' th' Stars fallin' like a shot as th' roof crashed in, an' where I'd left poor Jack was nothin' but a leppin' spout o' flame!

82

Bessie (*with partly repressed vehemence*) Ay, you left him! You twined his Rosary beads round his fingers, an' then you run like a hare to get out o' danger!

Capt. Brennan I took me chance as well as him . . . He took it like a man. His last whisper was to 'Tell Nora to be brave; that I'm ready to meet my God, an' that I'm proud to die for Ireland.' An' when our General heard it he said that 'Commandant Clitheroe's end was a gleam of glory.' Mrs Clitheroe's grief will be a joy when she realizes that she has had a hero for a husband.

Bessie If you only seen her, you'd know to th' differ.

Nora appears at door, left. She is clad only in her nightdress; her hair, uncared for some days, is hanging in disorder over her shoulders. Her pale face looks paler still because of a vivid red spot on the tip of each cheek. Her eyes are glimmering with the light of incipient insanity; her hands are nervously fiddling with her nightgown. She halts at the door for a moment, looks vacantly around the room, and then comes slowly in. The rest do not notice her till she speaks.

Nora (*in a quiet and monotonous tone*) No . . . Not there, Jack . . . I can feel comfortable only in our own familiar place beneath th' bramble tree . . . We must be walking for a long time; I feel very, very tired . . . Have we to go farther, or have we passed it by? (*Passing her hand across her eye*) Curious mist on my eyes . . . Why don't you hold my hand, Jack . . . (*Excitedly*) No, no, Jack, it's not. Can't you see it's a goldfinch. Look at th' black-satiny wings with th' gold bars, an' th' splash of crimson on its head . . . (*Wearily*) Something ails me, something ails me . . . Don't kiss me like that; you take my breath away, Jack . . . Why do you frown at me? . . . You're going away, and (*frightened*) I can't follow you.

83

Something's keeping me from moving . . . (*Crying out*) Jack, Jack, Jack!

Bessie (*who has gone over and caught Nora's arm*) Now, Mrs Clitheroe, you're a terrible woman to get up out of bed . . . You'll get cold if you stay here in them clothes.

Nora Cold? I'm feelin' very cold; it's chilly out here in th' counthry . . . (*Looking around frightened*) What place is this? Where am I?

Bessie (*coaxingly*) You're all right, Nora; you're with friends, an' in a safe place. Don't you know your uncle an' your cousin, an poor oul' Fluther?

Peter (*about to go over to Nora*) Nora, darlin', now –

Fluther (*pulling him back*) Now, leave her to Bessie, man. A crowd'll only make her worse.

Nora (*thoughtfully*) There is something I want to remember, an' I can't. (*With agony*) I can't, I can't, I can't! My head, my head! (*Suddenly breaking from Bessie, and running over to the men, and gripping Fluther by the shoulders*) Where is it? Where's my baby? Tell me where you've put it, where've you hidden it? My baby, my baby; I want my baby! My head, my poor head . . . Oh, I can't tell what is wrong with me. (*Screaming*) Give him to me, give me my husband!

Bessie Blessin' o' God on us, isn't this pitiful!

Nora (*struggling with Bessie*) I won't go away for you; I won't. Not till you give me back my husband. (*Screaming*) Murderers, that's what yous are; murderers, murderers!

Bessie S-s-sh. We'll bring Mr Clitheroe back to you, if you'll only lie down an' stop quiet . . . (*Trying to lead her in*) Come on, now, Nora, an' I'll sing something to you.

Nora I feel as if my life was thryin' to force its way out of my body . . . I can hardly breathe . . . I'm frightened, I'm frightened, I'm frightened! For God's sake, don't leave me, Bessie. Hold my hand, put your arms around me!

Fluther (*to Brennan*) Now you can see th' way she is, man.

Peter An' what way would she be if she heard Jack had gone west?

The Covey (*to Peter*) Shut up, you, man!

Bessie (*to Nora*) We'll have to be brave, an' let patience clip away th' heaviness of th' slow-movin' hours, rememberin' that sorrow may endure for th' night, but joy cometh in th' mornin' . . . Come on in, an' I'll sing to you, an' you'll rest quietly.

Nora (*stopping suddenly on her way to the room*) Jack an' me are goin' out somewhere this evenin'. Where I can't tell. Isn't it curious I can't remember . . . Maura, Maura, Jack, if th' baby's a girl; any name you like, if th' baby's a boy! . . . He's there. (*Screaming*) He's there, an' they won't give him back to me!

Bessie S-ss-s-h, darlin', s-ssh. I won't sing to you, if you're not quiet.

Nora (*nervously holding Bessie*) Hold my hand, hold my hand, an' sing to me, sing to me!

Bessie Come in an' lie down, an' I'll sing to you.

Nora (*vehemently*) Sing to me, sing to me; sing, sing!

Bessie (*singing as she leads Nora into room*)
Lead, kindly light, amid th' encircling gloom,
   Lead Thou me on.
Th' night is dark an' I am far from home,
   Lead Thou me on.

Keep Thou my feet, I do not ask to see
Th' distant scene – one step enough for me.

So long that Thou hast blessed me, sure Thou still
  Wilt lead me on . . .

They go in.

(*Singing in room*)
  O'er moor an' fen, o'er crag an' torrent, till
    Th' night is gone.
  An' in th' morn those angel faces smile
  That I have lov'd long since, an' lost awhile!

The Covey (*to Brennan*) Now that you've seen how bad she is, an' that we daren't tell her what has happened till she's betther, you'd best be slippin' back to where you come from.

Capt. Brennan There's no chance o' slippin' back now, for th' military are everywhere: a fly couldn't get through. I'd never have got here, only I managed to change me uniform for what I'm wearin' . . . I'll have to take me chance, an' thry to lie low here for a while.

The Covey (*frightened*) There's no place here to lie low. Th' Tommies 'll be hoppin' in here, any minute!

Peter (*aghast*) An' then we'd all be shanghaied!

The Covey Be God, there's enough afther happenin' to us!

Fluther (*warningly, as he listens*) Whisht, whisht, th' whole o' yous. I think I heard th' clang of a rifle butt on th' floor of th' hall below. (*All alertness*) Here, come on with th' cards again. I'll deal. (*He shuffles and deals the cards to all.*) Clubs up. (*To Brennan*) Thry to keep your hands from shakin', man. You lead, Peter.

As Peter throws out a card.

Four o' Hearts led.

The door opens and Corporal Stoddart of the Wiltshires enters in full war kit: steel helmet, rifle and bayonet, and trench tool. He looks round the room. A pause and a palpable silence.

(*Breaking the silence*) Two tens an' a five.

Corporal Stoddart 'Ello. (*Indicating the coffin*) This the stiff?

The Covey Yis.

Corporal Stoddart Who's gowing with it? Ownly one allowed to gow with it, you know.

The Covey I dunno.

Corporal Stoddart You dunnow?

The Covey I dunno.

Bessie (*coming into the room*) She's afther slippin' off to sleep again, thanks be to God. I'm hardly able to keep me own eyes open. (*To the soldier*) Oh, are yous goin' to take away poor little Mollser?

Corporal Stoddart Ay; 'oo's agowing with 'er?

Bessie Oh, th' poor mother, o' course. God help her, it's a terrible blow to her!

Fluther A terrible blow? Sure, she's in her element now, woman, mixin' earth to earth, an' ashes t' ashes an' dust to dust, an' revellin' in plumes an' hearses, last days an' judgements!

Bessie (*falling into chair by the fire*) God bless us! I'm jaded!

Corporal Stoddart Was she plugged?

The Covey Ah, no; died o' consumption.

Corporal Stoddart Ow, is that all? Thought she moight 'ave been plugged.

The Covey Is that all? Isn't it enough? D'ye know, comrade, that more die o' consumption than are killed in th' wars? An' it's all because of th' system we're livin' undher?

Corporal Stoddart Ow, I know. I'm a Sowcialist moiself, but I 'as to do my dooty.

The Covey (*ironically*) Dooty! Th' only dooty of a Socialist is th' emancipation of th' workers.

Corporal Stoddart Ow, a man's a man, an 'e 'as to foight for 'is country, 'asn't 'e?

Fluther (*aggressively*) You're not fightin' for your counthry here, are you?

Peter (*anxiously to Fluther*) Ay, ay, Fluther, none o' that, none o' that!

The Covey Fight for your counthry! Did y'ever read, comrade, Jenersky's *Thesis on the Origin, Development, an' Consolidation of th' Evolutionary Idea of the Proletariat?*

Corporal Stoddart Ow, cheese it, Paddy, cheese it!

Bessie (*sleepily*) How is things in th' town, Tommy?

Corporal Stoddart Ow, I fink it's nearly hover. We've got 'em surrounded, and we're clowsing in on the bloighters. Ow, it was only a little bit of a dawg-fight.

The sharp ping of the sniper's rifle is heard, followed by a squeal of pain.

Voices (*to the left in a chant*) Red Cr . . . oss, Red Cr . . . oss! Ambu . . . lance, Ambu . . . lance!

Corporal Stoddart (*excitedly*) Christ, that's another of our men 'it by that blawsted sniper! 'E's knocking abaht 'ere, somewheres. Gawd, when we gets th' bloighter, we'll give 'im the cold steel, we will. We'll jab the belly aht of 'im, we will!

> *Mrs Gogan comes in tearfully, and a little proud of the importance of being directly connected with death.*

Mrs Gogan (*to Fluther*) I'll never forget what you done for me, Fluther, goin' around at th' risk of your life settlin' everything with th' undhertaker an' th' cemetery people. When all me own were afraid to put their noses out, you plunged like a good one through hummin' bullets, an' they knockin' fire out o' th' road, tinklin' through th' frightened windows, an' splashin' themselves to pieces on th' walls! An' you'll find that Mollser, in th' happy place she's gone to, won't forget to whisper, now an' again, th' name o' Fluther.

Corporal Stoddart Git it aht, mother, git it aht.

Bessie (*from the chair*) It's excusin' me you'll be, Mrs Gogan, for not stannin' up, seein' I'm shaky on me feet for want of a little sleep, an' not desirin' to show any disrespect to poor little Mollser.

Fluther Sure, we all know, Bessie, that it's vice versa with you.

Mrs Gogan (*to Bessie*) Indeed, it's meself that has well chronicled, Mrs Burgess, all your gentle hurryin's to me little Mollser, when she was alive, bringin' her somethin' to dhrink, or somethin' t'eat, an' never passin' her without liftin' up her heart with a delicate word o' kindness.

Corporal Stoddart (*impatiently, but kindly*) Git it aht, git it aht, mother.

The Covey, Fluther, Brennan, and Peter carry out the coffin, followed by Mrs Gogan.

(*To Bessie, who is almost asleep*) 'Ow many men is in this 'ere 'ouse?

No answer.

(*Loudly*) 'Ow many men is in this 'ere 'ouse?

Bessie (*waking with a start*) God, I was nearly asleep! . . . How many men? Didn't you see them?

Corporal Stoddart Are they all that are in the 'ouse?

Bessie Oh, there's none higher up, but there may be more lower down. Why?

Corporal Stoddart All men in the district 'as to be rounded up. Somebody's giving 'elp to the snipers, and we 'as to take precautions. If I 'ad my woy, I'd make 'em all join hup, and do their bit! But I suppowse they and you are all Shinners.

Bessie (*who has been sinking into sleep, waking up to a sleepy vehemence*) Bessie Burgess is no Shinner, an' never had no thruck with anything spotted be th' fingers o' th' Fenians; but always made it her business to harness herself for Church whenever she knew that God Save the King was goin' to be sung at t'end of th' service; whose only son went to th' front in th' first contingent of the Dublin Fusiliers, an' that's on his way home carryin' a shatthered arm that he got fightin' for his King an' counthry!

Her head sinks slowly forward again. Peter comes into the room; his body is stiffened and his face is wearing a comically indignant look. He walks to and fro at the back of the room, evidently repressing a violent desire to speak angrily. He is followed in by

*Fluther, the Covey, and Brennan, who slinks into an
obscure corner of the room, nervous of notice.*

Fluther (*after an embarrassing pause*) Th' air in th' sthreet
outside's shakin' with the firin' o' rifles an' machine-
guns. It must be a hot shop in th' middle o' th' scrap.

Corporal Stoddart We're pumping lead in on 'em from
every side, now; they'll soon be shoving up th' white
flag.

Peter (*with a shout*) I'm tellin' you either o' yous two
lowsers 'ud make a betther hearse-man than Peter;
proddin' an' pokin' at me an' I helpin' to carry out a
corpse!

Fluther It wasn't a very derogatory thing for th' Covey
to say that you'd make a fancy hearse-man, was it?

Peter (*furiously*) A pair o' redjesthered bowseys
pondherin' from mornin' till night on how they'll get a
chance to break a gap through th' quiet nature of a man
that's always endeavourin' to chase out of him any
sthray thought of venom against his fella-man!

The Covey Oh, shut it, shut it, shut it!

Peter As long as I'm a livin' man, responsible for me
thoughts, words, an' deeds to th' Man above, I'll feel
meself instituted to fight again' th' sliddherin' ways of a
pair o' picaroons, whisperin', concurrin', concoctin', an'
conspirin' together to rendher me unconscious of th' life
I'm thryin' to live!

Corporal Stoddart (*dumbfounded*) What's wrong,
Daddy; wot 'ave they done to you?

Peter (*savagely to the Corporal*) You mind your own
business! What's it got to do with you, what's wrong
with me?

Bessie (*in a sleepy murmur*) Will yous thry to conthrol yourselves into quietness? Yous 'll waken her . . . up . . . on . . . me . . . again. (*She sleeps.*)

Fluther Come on, boys, to th' cards again, an' never mind him.

Corporal Stoddart No use of you gowing to start cawds; you'll be gowing out of 'ere, soon as Sergeant comes.

Fluther Goin' out o' here? An' why're we goin' out o' here?

Corporal Stoddart All men in district to be rounded up, and 'eld in till the scrap is hover.

Fluther An' where're we goin' to be held in?

Corporal Stoddart They're puttin 'em in a church.

The Covey A church?

Fluther What sort of a church? Is it a Protestan' church?

Corporal Stoddart I dunnow; I suppowse so.

Fluther (*dismayed*) Be God, it'll be a nice thing to be stuck all night in a Protestan' church!

Corporal Stoddart Bring the cawds; you moight get a chance of a goime.

Fluther Ah, no, that wouldn't do . . . I wondher? (*After a moment's thought*) Ah, I don't think we'd be doin' anything derogatory be playin' cards in a Protestan' church.

Corporal Stoddart If I was you I'd bring a little snack with me; you moight be glad of it before the mawning. (*Sings.*)

I do loike a snoice mince poy,
I do loike a snoice mince poy!

The snap of the sniper's rifle rings out again, followed simultaneously by a scream of pain. Corporal Stoddart goes pale, and brings his rifle to the ready, listening.

Voices (*chanting to the right*) Red Cro . . . ss, Red Cro . . . ss! Ambu . . . lance, Ambu . . . lance!

Sergeant Tinley comes in rapidly, pale, agitated, and fiercely angry.

Corporal Stoddart (*to Sergeant*) One of hour men 'it, Sergeant?

Sergeant Tinley Private Taylor; got 'it roight through the chest, 'e did; an 'ole in front of 'im as 'ow you could put your fist through, and 'arf 'is back blown awoy! Dum-dum bullets they're using. Gang of hassassins potting at us from behind roofs. That's not playing the goime: why down't they come into the owpen and foight fair!

Fluther (*unable to stand the slight*) Fight fair! A few hundhred scrawls o' chaps with a couple o' guns an' Rosary beads, again' a hundhred thousand thrained men with horse, fut, an' artillery . . . an' he wants us to fight fair! (*To Sergeant*) D'ye want us to come out in our skins an' throw stones!

Sergeant Tinley (*to Corporal*) Are these four all that are 'ere?

Corporal Stoddart Four; that's all, Sergeant.

Sergeant Tinley (*vindictively*) Come on, then; get the blighters aht. (*To the men*) 'Ere, 'op it aht! Aht into the streets with you, and if a snoiper sends another of our men west, you gow with 'im! (*He catches Fluther by the shoulder.*) Gow on, git aht!

Fluther Eh, who are you chuckin', eh?

Sergeant Tinley (*roughly*) Gow on, git aht, you blighter.

Fluther Who are you callin' a blighter to, eh? I'm a Dublin man, born an' bred in th' city, see?

Sergeant Tinley I down't care if you were Broin Buroo; git aht, git aht.

Fluther (*halting as he is going out*) Jasus, you an' your guns! Leave them down, an' I'd beat th' two o' yous without sweatin'!

Peter, Brennan, the Covey, and Fluther, followed by the soldiers, go out. Bessie is sleeping heavily on the chair by the fire. After a pause, Nora appears at door, left, in her nightdress. Remaining at door for a few moments she looks vaguely around the room. She then comes in quietly, goes over to the fire, pokes it, and puts the kettle on. She thinks for a few moments, pressing her hand to her forehead. She looks questioningly at the fire, and then at the press at back. She goes to the press, opens it, takes out a soiled cloth and spreads it on the table. She then places things for tea on the table.

Nora I imagine th' room looks very odd somehow . . . I was nearly forgetting Jack's tea . . . Ah, I think I'll have everything done before he gets in . . . (*She lilts gently, as she arranges the table.*)

Th' violets were scenting th' woods, Nora,
    Displaying their charms to th' bee,
When I first said I lov'd only you, Nora,
    An' you said you lov'd only me.

Th' chestnut blooms gleam'd through th' glade, Nora,
    A robin sang loud from a tree,
When I first said I lov'd only you, Nora,
    An' you said you lov'd only me.

She pauses suddenly, and glances round the room.

(*Doubtfully*) I can't help feelin' this room very strange . . .
what is it? . . . What is it? . . . I must think . . . I must
thry to remember . . .

Voices (*chanting in a distant street*) Ambu . . . lance,
Ambu . . . lance! Red Cro . . . ss, Red Cro . . . ss!

Nora (*startled and listening for a moment, then resuming
the arrangement of the table*)
    Trees, birds, an' bees sang a song, Nora,
      Of happier transports to be,
    When I first said I lov'd only you, Nora,
      An' you said you lov'd only me.

    *A burst of rifle fire is heard in a street near by,
    followed by the rapid tok, tok, tok of a machine-gun.*

(*Staring in front of her and screaming*) Jack, Jack, Jack!
My baby, my baby, my baby!

Bessie (*waking with a start*) You divil, are you afther
gettin' out o' bed again!

    *She rises and runs towards Nora, who rushes to the
    window, which she frantically opens.*

Nora (*at window, screaming*) Jack, Jack, for God's sake,
come to me!

Soldiers (*outside, shouting*) Git away, git away from that
window, there!

Bessie (*seizing hold of Nora*) Come away, come away,
woman, from that window!

Nora (*struggling with Bessie*) Where is it; where have
you hidden it? Oh, Jack, Jack, where are you?

Bessie (*imploringly*) Mrs Clitheroe, for God's sake, come
away!

Nora (*fiercely*) I won't; he's below. Let . . . me . . . go!

You're thryin' to keep me from me husband. I'll follow him. Jack, Jack, come to your Nora!

Bessie Hus-s-sh, Nora, Nora! He'll be here in a minute. I'll bring him to you, if you'll only be quiet – honest to God, I will.

With a great effort Bessie pushes Nora away from the window, the force used causing her to stagger against it herself. Two rifle shots ring out in quick succession. Bessie jerks her body convulsively; stands stiffly for a moment, a look of agonized astonishment on her face, then she staggers forward, leaning heavily on the table with her hands.

(*With an arrested scream of fear and pain*) Merciful God, I'm shot, I'm shot, I'm shot! . . . Th' life's pourin' out o' me! (*To Nora*) I've got this through . . . through you . . . through you, you bitch, you! . . . O God, have mercy on me! . . . (*To Nora*) You wouldn't stop quiet, no, you wouldn't, you wouldn't, blast you! Look at what I'm afther gettin', look at what I'm afther gettin' . . . I'm bleedin' to death, an' no one's here to stop th' flowin' blood! (*Calling*) Mrs Gogan, Mrs Gogan! Fluther, Fluther, for God's sake, somebody, a doctor, a doctor!

She staggers frightened towards the door, to seek for aid, but, weakening half-way across the room, she sinks to her knees, and bending forward, supports herself with her hands resting on the floor. Nora is standing rigidly with her back to the wall opposite, her trembling hands held out a little from the sides of her body, her lips quivering, her breast heaving, staring wildly at the figure of Bessie.

Nora (*in a breathless whisper*) Jack, I'm frightened . . . I'm frightened, Jack . . . Oh, Jack, where are you?

Bessie (*moaningly*) This is what's afther comin' on me for nursin' you day an' night . . . I was a fool, a fool, a fool!

Get me a dhrink o' wather, you jade, will you? There's a
fire burnin' in me blood! (*Pleadingly*) Nora, Nora, dear,
for God's sake, run out an' get Mrs Gogan, or Fluther, or
somebody to bring a doctor, quick, quick, quick!

Nora does not stir.

Blast you, stir yourself, before I'm gone!

Nora Oh, Jack, Jack, where are you?

Bessie (*in a whispered moan*) Jesus Christ, me sight's
goin'! It's all dark, dark! Nora, hold me hand! (*Bessie's
body lists over and she sinks into a prostrate position on
the floor.*) I'm dyin', I'm dyin' . . . I feel it . . . Oh God,
oh God! (*She feebly sings.*)

I do believe, I will believe
    That Jesus died for me;
That on th' cross He shed His blood,
    From sin to set me free . . .

I do believe . . . I will believe
    . . . Jesus died . . . me;
. . . th' cross He shed . . . blood,
    From sin . . . free.

*She ceases singing, and lies stretched out, still and very
rigid. A pause. Then Mrs Gogan runs in hastily.*

Mrs Gogan (*quivering with fright*) Blessed be God,
what's after happenin'? (*To Nora*) What's wrong, child,
what's wrong? (*She sees Bessie, runs to her and bends
over the body.*) Bessie, Bessie! (*She shakes the body.*)
Mrs Burgess, Mrs Burgess! (*She feels Bessie's forehead.*)
My God, she's as cold as death. They're afther murdherin'
th' poor inoffensive woman!

*Sergeant Tinley and Corporal Stoddart enter
agitatedly, their rifles at the ready.*

Sergeant Tinley (*excitedly*) This is the 'ouse. That's the window!

Nora (*pressing back against the wall*) Hide it, hide it; cover it up, cover it up!

Sergeant Tinley (*going over to the body*) 'Ere, what's this? Who's this? (*Looking at Bessie*) Oh Gawd, we've plugged one of the women of the 'ouse.

Corporal Stoddart Whoy the 'ell did she gow to the window? Is she dead?

Sergeant Tinley Oh, dead as bedamned. Well, we couldn't afford to toike any chawnces.

Nora (*screaming*) Hide it, hide it; don't let me see it! Take me away, take me away, Mrs Gogan!

Mrs Gogan runs into room, left, and runs out again with a sheet which she spreads over the body of Bessie.

Mrs Gogan (*as she spreads the sheet*) Oh, God help her, th' poor woman, she's stiffenin' out as hard as she can! Her face has written on it th' shock o' sudden agony, an' her hands is whitenin' into th' smooth shininess of wax.

Nora (*whimperingly*) Take me away, take me away; don't leave me here to be lookin' an' lookin' at it!

Mrs Gogan (*going over to Nora and putting her arm around her*) Come on with me, dear, an' you can doss in poor Mollser's bed, till we gather some neighbours to come an' give th' last friendly touches to Bessie in th' lonely layin' of her out.

Mrs Gogan and Nora go out slowly.

Corporal Stoddart (*who has been looking around, to Sergeant Tinley*) Tea here, Sergeant. Wot abaht a cup of scald?

Sergeant Tinley Pour it aht, Stoddart, pour it aht. I could scoff hanything just now.

Corporal Stoddart pours out two cups of tea, and the two soldiers begin to drink. In the distance is heard a bitter burst of rifle and machine-gun fire, interspersed with the boom, boom of artillery. The glare in the sky seen through the window flares into a fuller and a deeper red.

There gows the general attack on the Powst Office.

Voices (*in a distant street*) Ambu . . . lance, Ambu . . . lance! Red Cro . . . ss, Red Cro . . . ss!

Voices of Soldiers (*at a barricade outside the house; singing*)
   They were summoned from the 'illside,
   They were called in from the glen,
   And the country found 'em ready
   At the stirring call for men.
   Let not tears add to their 'ardship,
   As the soldiers pass along,
   And although our 'eart is breaking,
   Make it sing this cheery song.

Sergeant Tinley *and* **Corporal Stoddart** (*joining in the chorus, as they sip the tea*)
   Keep the 'owme fires burning,
   While your 'earts are yearning;
   Though your lads are far away
   They dream of 'owme;
   There's a silver loining
   Through the dark cloud shoining,
   Turn the dark cloud inside out,
   Till the boys come 'owme!

   Curtain.

Textual Notes

5   Maggie – elsewhere Mrs Gogan's first name is given as Jenny and Cissie, a sign of the playwright carelessly at work.

6   derogatory – critical, ascribing blame. But Fluther uses the word to suit all occasions.

7   foostherin' – bustling about fussily (Dolan, *Dictionary of Hiberno-English*).

8   canonicals – clerical dress. Presumably Mrs Gogan means 'regimentals' or military dress.

–   Citizen Army – the Irish Citizen Army was founded by Jim Larkin in November 1913 as a defence force for the Dublin workers during the great lock-out of 1913–14. O'Casey was the secretary for a time.

–   Liberty Hall – headquarters of the Irish Transport and General Workers' Union and of the Irish Citizen Army, located in Beresford Place.

9   figaries – Mrs Gogan possibly means 'filigree', ornamental work. 'Figary' (Hiberno-English) could mean 'stylish clothing' (Dolan, *Dictionary of Hiberno-English*).

11   Covey – a smart alec, a know-all person (Ayling, *Seven Plays*, glossary).

—   Plough an' th' Stars – the banner of the Irish Citizen Army.

—   *in seculo seculorum* – for all eternity.

12   cunundhrums – conundrums, riddles. Here and throughout (compare 'mollycewels' for 'molecules' or 'wurum' for 'worm') O'Casey renders Dublin speech phonetically.

14   Georgina: The Sleepin' Vennis – *The Sleeping Venus* by Giorgione, sixteenth-century Italian painter.

16   Dear harp o' me counthry – one of the popular melodies of the Irish poet and songwriter Thomas Moore (1779–1852).

17   where your bowsey battlin' 'll meet, maybe, with an encore – where your drunken fighting may be welcome. (Note the theatrical term 'encore'.)

18   Jenersky's *Thesis* – a fictional Marxist text.

—   whole – complete. The phrase is Dublinese, 'a great fellow'.

19   a glass o' malt – whiskey.

20   to speak proud things, an' lookin' like a mighty one – a possible quotation from the Bible, untraced.

—   g'up ower o' that – go away. Nora's rather refined speech here lapses into colloquialism (the phrase is spoken as one word); ower – 'out'.

21   sorra – no (Hiberno-English, emphatic negative).

—   *the Foresters* – according to O'Casey, 'The Irish National Foresters is merely a benevolent Society, and those who wear the costume worn by Peter are a subject of amusement to intelligent Irishmen' (French's acting edition, 1932, p. 80).

23   Oh, where's th' slave so lowly – another of Moore's *Irish Melodies*, 1807.

24   varmint – vermin (Ayling, *Seven Plays*, glossary).

31   *The Soldiers' Song* – by Peadar Kearney (1883–1942), first published in 1912, later the Irish national anthem.

32   yous'll not escape from th' arrow that flieth be night – quotation from the Bible, Psalms 91: 5.

—   titther – tittle, particle.

34   Curse o' God on th' haporth – Dublin slang for 'nothing at all'; 'haporth' – halfpenny-worth.

—   It is a glorious thing . . . of them! – lines taken from 'The Coming Revolution' (1913), a speech by Pádraic Pearse (1879–1916), leader of the Irish Volunteers.

35   gems – possibly 'gentlemen' (ironic).

—   dhrink Loch Erinn dhry – colloquial expression for great thirst; presumably referring to Lough Erne in Co. Fermanagh.

—   Wolfe Tone – Theobald Wolfe Tone (1763–98), founder of the United Irishmen, whose grave in Bodenstown, Co. Kildare, became a shrine for republicans from the centenary of Tone's death in 1898. See also the note to p. 40.

36   vice versa – the opposite way.

—   Comrade soldiers . . . country – lines from 'Peace and the Gael' (1915), a speech by Pádraic Pearse. The next sentence in the speech here is O'Casey's addition. It may be noted that Pearse's speech was delivered in *December* 1915, one month after O'Casey's specified time for Act Two.

39   shinannickin' afther Judies – chasing girls. The word 'shenanigans', or 'shinannickin', is usually a noun meaning, colloquially, 'mischievous behaviour, trickery' (Dolan, *Dictionary of Hiberno-English*).

40   Bodenstown – site of cemetery in Co. Kildare where the grave of Theobald Wolfe Tone is located (see note to p. 35).

41   little Catholic Belgium – the point here is that Bessie is a staunch Protestant with a son fighting in France.

42   flappers – flighty society girls.

—   a woman that is loud an' stubborn . . . house – a qotation from the Bible, Proverbs 7: 11. The reference is to a 'harlot' or whore.

43   Cissie Gogan – compare 'Maggie' (p. 5) and 'Jenny' (p. 44).

—   The last sixteen months . . . God! – a second quotation from Pádraic Pearse's speech 'Peace and the Gael' (1915).

—   Saint Vincent de Paul – a charitable organisation which gives vouchers to the poor for food and clothing.

44   precept upon precept . . . little – a quotation from the Bible, Isaiah 28: 10. The passage is an attack on drunkards.

—   weddin' lines – marriage certificate (Ayling, *Seven Plays*, glossary).

—   Jinnie Gogan – earlier (p. 43), Mrs Gogan gave her first name as Cissie and at the outset (p. 5) as 'Maggie'. O'Casey was not usually careless over such details.

45   dawny – frail.

47   gom – a silly, a foolish person (Dolan, *Dictionary of Hiberno-English*).

48   chiselur – child (usually spelt 'chiseller', Dublin slang).

—   Shan Van Vok – Fluther's rendering of the Gaelic, *Sean Bhean Bhocht*, or 'poor old woman', i.e., Ireland.

51   bowsey – a disreputable drunkard; Dublin slang, perhaps related to 'booze' (Dolan, *Dictionary of Hiberno-English*).

52   malignifed – Fluther means 'maligned', insulted.

—   clatther – blow (Hiberno-English).

53   Our foes are strong . . . peace! – from Pádraic Pearse's 'O'Donovan Rossa – Graveside Oration' (1915).

54   I once had a lover . . . th' bed! – Rosie's song was cut from the first production in 1926 at the horrified insistence of the government representative on the Abbey Board.

56   put much pass on – take much notice of.

—   aself – itself, i.e. 'even'.

57   GPO – the General Post Office in O'Connell Street, headquarters of the 1916 Rising.

58   gunboat *Helga* – the *Helga* did not come up the Liffey until the Wednesday of Easter Week, the Rising having begun on Monday.

—   shanghaied – forced into a situation from which there is no escape.

—   th' boyo – Uncle Peter.

58 Orange – Mrs Burgess is a Protestant and unionist, which
may be enough to identify her with the Orange Society in
Northern Ireland (founded 1794 as a defence organisation
dedicated to that first great loyalist King William of Orange
(1650–1702)). Thus, here, 'Orange' means 'loyalist'.

59 Sorra mend th' lasses – bad luck to the women (Dublinese).

62 only for – if it wasn't for.

— th' tossers – the coins and strip of wood with which to play
'pitch-and-toss'. The men would bet on whether the coins
came up 'heads' or 'harps' (tails), the two sides of the Irish
coinage.

— oul' son – a friendly greeting, gender-neutral.

63 a juice . . . a tanner – two (old) pence, and six (old) pence.
Before decimalisation in 1971 there were twelve pennies
in a shilling and hence a special coin for sixpence, half a
shilling.

64 th' Volunteers – that is, those in O'Connell Street, who fired
on the Irish themselves in an attempt to stop the looting
(compare pp. 70–71).

65 Wrathmines – the fashionable suburb of Rathmines, its
higher class designated by the fancy (British) pronunciation.

68 from backside to breakfast time – a Dublin expression:
inside out.

— kinch – twist (Ayling, *Seven Plays*, glossary).

— sorra mind I'd mind – I wouldn't mind in the least ('sorra' =
sorrow = strong negative).

— met with a dhrop – got a shock.

69 mot – girl (Dublin slang).

72 The Minsthrel Boys – the patriots. The reference is to
Thomas Moore's poem, 'The Minstrel Boy to the war is
gone', *Irish Melodies*, 1807.

77 shelter me safely in th' shadow of Thy wings – from Psalms
91: 4.

79 a nose – suspicion.

— pimpin' – spying.

— Danes . . . Brian Boru – in 1014 Brian Boru, high king of
Ireland, won a decisive battle against the Danes at Clontarf.

— Spuds up again – spades are trumps again. They are playing
'twenty-five'.

80 hand runnin' – in succession.

85 gone west – dead. The phrase was much used during World
War I.

TEXTUAL NOTES

—   sorrow may endure . . . mornin' – a quotation from the
Bible, Psalms 30: 5. O'Casey replaced 'weeping' with
'sorrow'.

—   Lead, kindly light – a hymn written in 1832 by John Henry
Cardinal Newman (1801–90), a convert well known to
Dubliners, since he founded the Catholic University (later
University College, Dublin) at St Stephen's Green in 1854.

88   a man's a man – echo of a poem by Robert Burns (1759–96),
'For a' that, and a' that'.

90   join hup – conscription was a controversial subject in
Ireland in 1916, but was successfully kept out.

—   Shinners – members of Sinn Féin.

91   redjesthered – registered (professional).

—   picaroons – thieves.

93   blighter – contemptible or annoying person.

99   They were summoned . . . 'owme! – the popular World War I
song by Ivor Novello (1893–1951).

REFERENCES

Ayling, Ronald, 'Notes' in *Seven Plays by Sean O'Casey: A Students'
Edition*, London: Macmillan, 1985.

Dolan, Terence Patrick, *A Dictionary of Hiberno-English: The
Irish Use of English*, Dublin: Gill and Macmillan, 1998.